RESTORING WOOD

RESTORING WOOD

Restoring Wood

Text:

Eva Pascual i Miró

Step by Step Projects:

Anna Jover i Armengol

Josep Maria Miret i Farré

English translation:

Michael Brunelle

Beatriz Cortabarria

Graphic design:

Josep Guasch

Photography:

Nos & Soto

Josep Pascual

Illustrations:

Antoni Vidal

Original title of the book in Spanish: *Restauración de Madera*
© Copyright Parramón Ediciones, S.A.—World Rights
Published by Parramón Ediciones, S.A., Barcelona, Spain.

Authors: Eva Pascual i Miró, Anna Jover i Armengol, and Josep Maria Miret i Farré.

The publisher would like to thank the artists, museums, and collectors who collaborated on this work.

All inquiries should be addressed to:
Barron's Educational Series, Inc.
250 Wireless Boulevard
Hauppauge, New York 11788
http://www.barronseduc.com

Library of Congress Catalog Card No.: 99-066826
International Standard Book No.: 0-7641-5223-8

Printed in Spain
987654321

Con

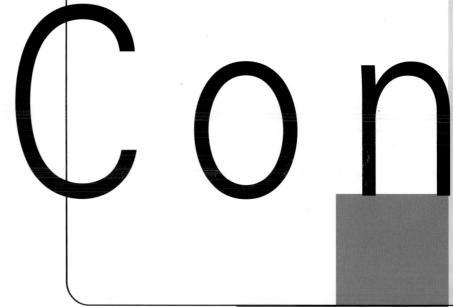

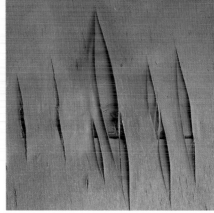

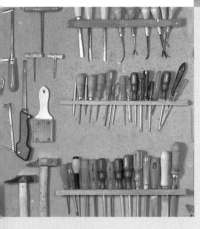

ents

Introduction

*T*his book is intended to be a practical manual for restoring wood objects. It is organized in a way that will allow the professional woodworker to find needed information, and it will also be a clear guide for those who wish to learn about restoring wood. The reader will be able to locate any desired chapter or subject based on his or her requirements and knowledge.

The manual is arranged in six chapters with detailed information on the materials and processes necessary for restoring wood.

The first chapter, a brief introduction to furniture history and styles, attempts to give a general overview of the chronological evolution of furniture to help the wood restorer place a furniture piece in its historical context.

The second chapter addresses damaged wood. It begins by analyzing the internal structures of wood and goes on to cover the factors that contribute to its deterioration. It also analyzes other factors of deterioration such as humidity, temperature, and light. Finally, some basic elements of preventive wood conservation are explained. Preventive conservation is, surely, the foundation and ally of restoration.

The third and fourth chapters are comprehensive summaries of the tools and materials that are used in all phases of the restoration process. The main focus is wood, and we begin with a practical guide to the species most commonly used in the manufacture of furniture and structures (and therefore in restoration), and a review of the most commonly available wood parts. Following that is an explanation of safety products and commonly used supplies arranged according to how they are used in restoration projects, the different types of tools, and the basic elements of shop layout. This section will be a useful reference in any kind of restoration project.

The fifth chapter is organized around practical examples and addresses the technical aspects of restoration. Here we demonstrate the complete approach applied to the restoration of wood: evaluation, preliminary processes, stripping, special treatments, carpentry, finishing, and assembly of the object. It is a script for the furniture restorer, describing the steps and the order to be followed before, during, and after the restoration process.

The sixth chapter is a step-by-step, practical guide to the restoration of different types of objects. They are ordered by level of difficulty, from simple to complex according to the processes that are required. Therefore, they begin with a simple carpentry project and end with the restoration of a finish. The examples in this chapter are in themselves unique, but the systems and processes are easily applied to any restoration task that the reader may face.

Finally, a glossary containing vocabulary specific to this field will be a helpful reference tool, and a bibliography is included for readers who wish to learn more about this subject.

This book does not presume to be the definitive manual on restoring wood; it is only an attempt to give a basic yet complete overview of a trade that requires study, much experience, humility when facing a piece of furniture, and constant learning. The aim of this book is to serve as a reference work for professionals and as an initiation for beginners in the field of wood restoration.

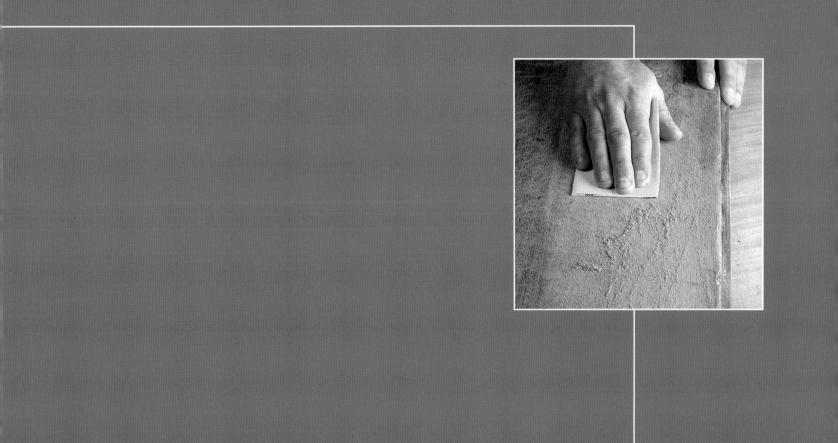

This book has been developed by a group of professionals working in fields related to wood restoration.

Eva Pascual i Miró has a degree in art history from the University of Barcelona. She specialized in Museum Studies, and Design and Restoration at the Polytechnic University of Catalonia and in Preventive Conservation at the Autonomous University of Catalonia. Following family tradition, she developed a knowledge of antiques, focusing mainly on medieval furnishings and particularly on Catalan furniture. Her professional path has taken her, among other places, to various museums and cultural institutions in Catalonia as a bibliographer, administrator of state-owned art treasures, and exhibit coordinator. She now directs and coordinates the Department of Restoration Materials and Preventive Conservation for a company that serves cultural institutions in Barcelona.

Anna Jover i Armengol has a degree in chemistry from the University of Barcelona. She specialized in underwater archeological restoration, particularly in wet wood, at the National Museum of Denmark in Copenhagen, and has written numerous articles on the subject. From its beginning, she has been a frequent collaborator with the Center for Underwater Archeology of Catalonia. She presently works in her own furniture restoration shop.

Josep Maria Miret i Farré is a fine furniture restorer specializing in period styles. He shares his vast knowledge of furniture restoration in private classes for fine arts professionals. On many occasions he has worked in Brittany (France) restoring church altarpieces. He is presently working in his own furniture restoration shop.

*T*o restore a wood object properly, it is necessary to know its history. This concept is fundamental to the success of any project regardless of how simple and easy it may be. For this reason, the first step in restoring a wood furniture piece is an analysis of its time period and the design and construction characteristics of the piece.

Most of the time the wood restorer is faced with furniture and decorative objects that are in need of repair. The history of furniture styles is mirrored in the evolution of the construction techniques. Knowledge of the evolution of furniture, both its style and its construction, will help suggest the approach to be taken in the restoration process. The first thing to note is how the object was constructed, which will indicate where it was made, the time period, the style, and its possible problems, such as additions or reconstruction, and so on. A complete study of the piece will let us make comparisons to similar pieces. This way we can obtain information about its use, and about the decorative elements, processes, and the finish of the furniture piece. We can also understand the way it was made, whether it is a traditional piece, or if it belongs to a more sophisticated style.

In this first chapter, we will limit ourselves to explaining some of the basics of construction and furniture styles in Europe. The wood restorer will have to use this as a point of departure to delve more deeply into the subject with the help of the numerous books available on the market.

A Brief History
of *Furniture*

A Brief History of Furniture

The history of furniture begins with and runs parallel to human history, insomuch as artifacts are an expression of humans and the periods of their history. Throughout history, furniture pieces have been much appreciated by and made for the ruling classes; they have not become available and produced for large segments of the population until relatively recently. These characteristics have favored the conservation and reutilization of the furniture.

Information about different kinds of furniture exists thanks to surviving artistic representations of them, mainly in paintings and sculpture. It seems that the first pieces of furniture developed by humans were meant for rest (chairs, thrones…) and to store goods (chests, boxes…). All of the information about furniture produced by ancient civilizations, from Mesopotamia until the Roman Empire, is incomplete. It is mainly obtained from indirect sources (graphic or written), and any examples that have actually survived until our times usually belong to a funerary and cult tradition (like the furniture pieces in Egyptian tombs); therefore, it is very risky to attempt to establish any stylistic affiliations.

The Middle Ages

The earliest pieces of furniture that exist in any number in Europe date from the Middle Ages. Two types stand out: storage pieces (chests and trunks) and court furniture (thrones and chairs for nobles.)

The construction methods of the early centuries were based on the use of thick planks roughly planed with an adze and held together with large pegged joints. This method resulted in heavy pieces in which the joints were nearly always reinforced with metal parts like wide hinges and nails. The construction methods dictated the form of the furniture. There is also furniture from the medieval period whose forms derived from the furniture of earlier periods, a clear example being the thrones and chairs of the Roman period where the Roman tradition still persisted. This type of furniture had a symbolic function that had little to do with its normal use.

Romanesque decoration was almost always based on carved geometric and painted motifs that helped decorate the heavy wood planks or hide joinery and construction elements.

During the Gothic period, there was a major change in furniture construction methods.

The use of the hydraulic saw (already known to the Romans) made available great quantities of thin planks, which lend themselves to elaborate joinery, and eliminated the need for heavily reinforced furniture pieces. It was the time when the various trade organizations established norms for the use and working of different materials. The carpenters and sawyers guilds became especially important in regions like Flanders. Decoration was based on the use of architectural motifs like finials, molding, and arches, among others. It became normal to hide the base material (wood) under polychrome and gilding, an approach that prevailed almost until the nineteenth century.

Tables and certain kinds of beds could be taken apart, and sometimes were as simple as planks laid across sawhorses.

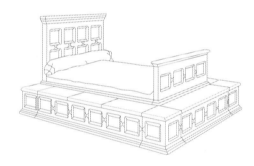

▲ **Gothic bed.** The chests around the bed are used for storage and support the bed. They are decorated with base moldings and panels. Italy.

◀ **Gothic folding chair.** Italy.

◀ **Romanesque throne.** The decoration is based on carvings that represent various animal motifs and geometric elements. Northern Europe.

◀ **Gothic wardrobe.** The front panels are decorated with pierced motifs. England.

◀ **Chest.** The panels are decorated with carved and painted scenes. The top forgoes its function in favor of its decorative value. Upper Adigio, Italy.

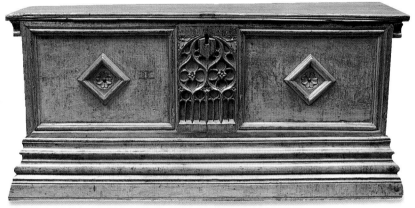

◄ **Gothic chair**. Made of panels held in place by a frame. Each panel has a carved linen fold motif. Flanders.

▶ **Gothic chest**. Storage piece made of four joined panels, plus the base and lid. Decorated with molding, diamonds, and baseboard. Catalonia, Spain.

The Renaissance

During the fifteenth century, while the Gothic furniture tradition continued to dominate in certain parts of Europe, the Renaissance was taking place in Italy. The return to classic sources that provoked the Renaissance revolution created a style based on proportions and a consistency in volumes added to a great constructive ability. New types of static furniture appeared during this period: the table and the bed. Some of them acquired monumental proportions, like the beds with headboards sitting on chests. These began to acquire an ornamental character that gave rise to complicated furniture. Wardrobes were not solely used as religious furniture as in the previous period.

During the sixteenth century, furniture lost the formal severity that dictated its structure and size. Furniture was decorated with exaggerated architectural elements that covered the surface with movement and contrast (*chiaroscuro*). Ornamental moldings, columns, and inlay were used.

A unique piece of furniture appeared on the Iberian Peninsula that later became popular throughout South America: the *vargueño*. (This was a storage piece with a table or chest for a base. The top part, sometimes called a desk, had a fold down front that sometimes acted as a writing surface.)

◄ **Renaissance chair**. The carved decoration on parts of the frame make this chair valuable. The fabric is preserved on the seat and backrest. Italy.

◄ **Renaissance credenza**. The credenza is possibly the first cupboard. It later evolved into the wardrobe and the cupboard. France.

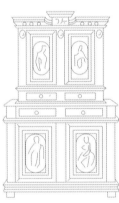

◄ **Renaissance wardrobe**. The structure and decoration of wardrobes followed the rules of classicism. Italy.

▶ **Renaissance bed**. A bed with four columns that support a canopy. The columns and carved decoration follow classic models. Italy.

▲ **Renaissance mirror**. The structure and decoration are based on architectural motifs in the classical tradition. Italy.

▼ **Renaissance table**. The decorative aspects are the turned crosspiece and the carved profile of the legs. Tuscany, Italy.

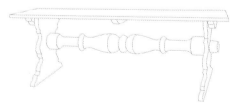

▶ **Chest, 16th century**. The fine inlay work on the drawers, top panel, and sides were inspired by traditional Mudejar furniture. Spain.

The Baroque

New types of furniture appeared during this period, like the console table, the chest of drawers, and the *canterano*. Furniture lost its stiff formality and became quite dramatic. Surfaces were convex, rippled, and curved, and profiles had a spiral form and broken cornices. In general, furniture adapted the same decorative elements as those used in architecture, like the spiral column. Gilded surfaces made their appearance, and there was a taste for heavy drapery.

Thanks to trade in the tropical zones, ebony became popular (in Holland), as did other exotic woods that were used for building furniture and as veneer for decorating surfaces.

The centralization of furniture production for the French Court resulted in the **Louis XIV** style. Its decorative repertoire included heads, trophies, wreaths, and suns, among other things, always following a strict symmetry. Legs had a curved profile and terminated in a lion's paw. Inlaid materials included silver, tortoise shell (in furniture made by André Charles Boulle), and gilt bronze. New furniture pieces were developed: the richly upholstered sofa and the wing chair.

The English **William and Mary** style combined the structure of Dutch furniture and the decoration of the Louis XIV style. The main characteristics of this furniture were its simplicity, bulkiness, and flat surfaces, but with the decorative repertoire of the Louis XIV style. The feet were made in the form of round or flattened balls.

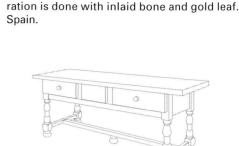

◀ *Vargueño,* **17th century.** Furniture piece consisting of a lower chest with drawers and an upper writing desk. The architectural decoration is done with inlaid bone and gold leaf. Spain.

▲ **Table, 17th century.** A work table with drawers. France.

◀ **Baroque bed.** This piece from the beginning of the Baroque period already shows the taste for theatrical, ostentatious, and overly elaborate decoration. Italy.

▲ **Baroque console.** The console made its appearance as an auxiliary piece that was so highly decorated that its lavishness took precedence over utility. Italy.

▶ *Vargueño.* The *vargueño* is a piece of furniture that combines the functions of a storage chest and a writing desk. Spain.

▶ **Baroque wardrobe.** The decorative and theatrical feeling is emphasized by the architectural decoration of the figures. Italy.

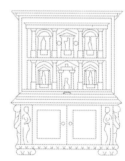

◀ **Table, 17th century.** Work table with heavily carved legs. The crosspiece has been replaced by two forged iron braces. Majorca, Spain.

▶ **Chair, 18th century.** Traditional chair. Possibly Majorcan. Spain.

The Eighteenth Century

In the eighteenth century, the style established during the Baroque period became highly exaggerated in the Rococo. Decoration was elaborate, profusely gilded, and painted. Although the importation of furniture by the East India Company was common in England and Holland from the seventeenth century, the Chinese style did not become popular in Europe until the middle of the eighteenth century. Popular demand resulted in the European manufacture of furniture with imitation lacquer. The major production centers were Venice, France, and England.

The taste for the Baroque faded in the **Louis XV** style. Rococo and shell motifs were used, and architectural decoration was discarded in favor of "S" curves and asymmetric and irregular motifs.

The **Chippendale** style got its name from the English cabinetmaker Thomas Chippendale. His furniture was known for its use of solid mahogany and satinwood. Unlike French furniture makers, he did not use gilt bronze pieces. He typically used fretwork designs inspired by Chinese and Gothic motifs in chair backs and library doors.

▲ **Rococo chair.** Carved decoration became exaggerated. France.

▼ **Wardrobe, 18th century.** A highly decorated piece with wavy carved scrolls and molding. Catalonia, Spain.

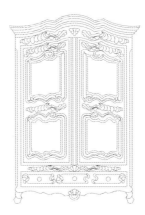

▲ **Writing desk, 18th century.** Work tables with stylish lines became popular. France.

▼ **Bench, 18th century.** Chippendale style with a ribbon band design. England.

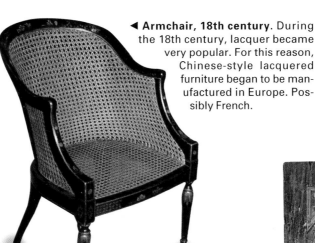

◄ **Armchair, 18th century.** During the 18th century, lacquer became very popular. For this reason, Chinese-style lacquered furniture began to be manufactured in Europe. Possibly French.

▲ **Mirror, 18th century.** Louis XV style. Possibly French.

► **Bench with backrest, 18th century.** Louis XV style. Catalonia, Spain.

► **Door, 18th century.** A vernacular piece with motifs adapted from the Rococo style. Spain.

▲ **Bed, 18th century.** The painted surfaces and gold leaf add to the decorative value of the piece. Catalonia, Spain.

▲ **Bed, late 18th century.** Louis XVI style. The headboard and footboard are upholstered. France.

▶ **Armchair, late 18th century.** Louis XVI style. Furniture forms return to Classicism. France.

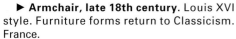

▼ **Chest of drawers, late 18th to early 19th century.** This piece shows the austere lines of the 19th century, although the inlay work still has the decorative feeling of the 18th. Catalonia, Spain.

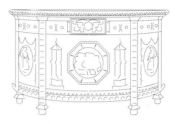

▲ **Chest, late 18th century.** Adam style, precursor of the neoclassic style. England.

▲ **Chest of drawers, late 18th century.** Charles IV style. Spain.

▲ **Chair, late 18th to early 19th century.** Neoclassic style. Spain.

The Nineteenth Century

The nineteenth century, like the twentieth century, was a period of great and rapid change in furniture all over Europe. The century began with Neoclassicism and ended with the free forms of Modernism. It was also when the mass production of furniture began. As a result of political changes in Europe, there was a return to ancient classic styles, influenced by the archeological discoveries of the time. The result was Neoclassicism, a return to furniture that was light, symmetrical and had stylized forms inspired by ancient Etruscan, Greek, Roman, and Egyptian styles. The decorative repertoire was based on the use of wreaths, borders, friezes, and claw feet.

In France, the **Louis XVI** style adapted the neoclassic look. Furniture returned to symmetrical forms and straight lines. Legs were made straight and fluted. The decoration centered on the use of wreaths, classical capitals, amorous symbols, and medallions. The most noble wood, mahogany, was left visible, and furniture dimensions were reduced.

The **Empire** style developed in France coinciding with the reign of Napoleon. It adapted the repertoire and characteristics of neoclassic furniture and featured heavy, solid proportions. The use of sphinxes, lion paws, swans, eagles, and laurel wreaths became

▼ **Desk, late 18th century.** Lacquered furniture was adapted to European taste, resulting in Oriental style lacquered pieces. France.

▲ **Dressing table, 18th–19th century.** A highly decorative feeling is achieved by the marquetry work and the finely finished legs. Catalonia, Spain.

▲ **Chair, 1902.** A Modernist piece designed by Antonio Gaudí for the Casa Calvet. Catalonia, Spain.

▲ **Bench, 19th century.** Empire style. During this period, sphinxes and chimeras became popular.

▲ **Wardrobe, 19th century.** Isabelline style, in which the taste for marquetry and sinuous forms stands out. Catalonia, Spain.

▲ **Bed, 19th century.** The sleigh bed became popular in the Empire style. Spain.

▶ **Dressing table, 19th century.** Empire style. Spain.

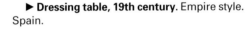

▶ **Bed, circa 1910.** A Modernist piece where the use of curved lines stands out. Catalonia, Spain.

▼ **Wardrobe, 19th century.** Alphonsine style, known for dark furniture with thick heavy molding.

widespread. The sleigh bed became popular, a bed with a semi-circular shape and a canopy that usually was placed with one side against the wall.

The **neo-Gothic** style and **Historicism** were reflections of mid-century thought, which advocated the return to the Middle Ages as the period of greatest splendor and as a reaction against the prevailing Classicism. These styles reconstructed the Gothic influence of the interiors created in France by Eugene Viollet-le-Duc. Furniture was created that adapted any aspect of the medieval vocabulary, mixing up styles and periods.

Thonet furniture was named for Michael Thonet, a Prussian cabinetmaker who patented a chemical-mechanical wood bending process in 1841. This technical innovation created a style that lasted until World War II and allowed furniture to be mass-produced at nearly industrial levels.

Modernism was the last grand style that influenced all of Europe. It had different names in different countries: *Art Nouveau* in France and Belgium, *Modern Style* in England, *Jugendstil* in Germany, and *Modernismo* in Spain, especially in Catalonia.

This style encompassed as many different works as authors, but all had in common the use of a sinuous line, free forms, and the combining of diverse materials and processes like mosaics, metalwork, and stained glass.

▲ **Chair, circa 1850.** Thonet chair, in solid bentwood. Germany.

▶ **Table, 19th century.** A table in the Isabelline style. Spain.

The wood that is such an important component of everyday objects like pieces of art or the most sophisticated scientific instruments deteriorates with the passage of time. The material itself is unstable; it has a tendency to break down or to transform itself into the basic elements found in nature or into more stable compounds.

There are well-known factors that initiate or accelerate the changes or deterioration of wood, causing the prejudicial modification of one or more of its characteristics. These factors are light, temperature, and humidity. The last two are closely related, as we will soon see. Organic materials, whether of vegetable origin (paper, wood, cotton, wicker, and so on) or animal origin (leather, wool, silk, wax, and so on) can cause physical and mechanical changes and become great allies of biological attacks. Inorganic materials (metals, mineral, stone, glass, ceramic, and so on) can produce chemical reactions that may contribute to physical changes depending on the condition of the wood, possible pathologies, and the characteristics of the wood itself.

Damaged Wood

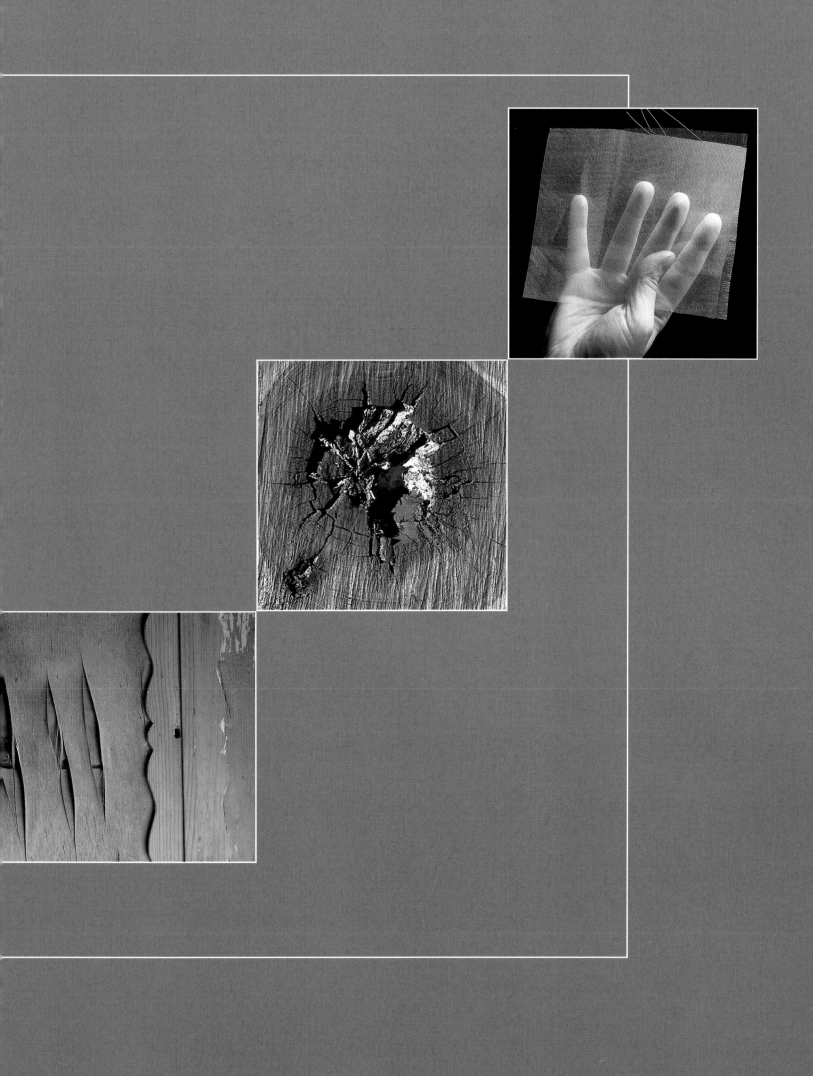

Wood

Wood is a structure of fibers that act as a support and allow the circulation of water and nutrients in large plants. Its composition is approximately 50% cellulose, 30% lignin, and 20% resins, starches, tannins, and sugars. These percentages vary depending on the species and the part of the plant.

Structurally, wood is made up of pith, heartwood, sapwood, inner bark, and bark. The pith is the center and together with the spongy layer surrounding it, constitutes the heart. The heartwood is the actual wood. The sapwood is the young wood of the tree, produced by its annual growth and, therefore, softer and paler than the older wood. The inner bark is the fabric that conducts the descending sap. The bark is the fiber that waterproofs and protects the tree.

The spring and autumn fibers form the annual growth rings. In the spring fibers, the veins that conduct the raw sap to the leaves dominate; they are light colored and are not very compact. The autumn fibers, with smaller, more compact veins, serve as support and have more color. The function of the ray is to conduct the sap to the outer part of the tree.

▲ Oak tree.

◀ Trunk section, where we can see the different parts: heartwood, sapwood, and bark. The pith has suffered some damage.

▼ Macroscopic structure of wood.

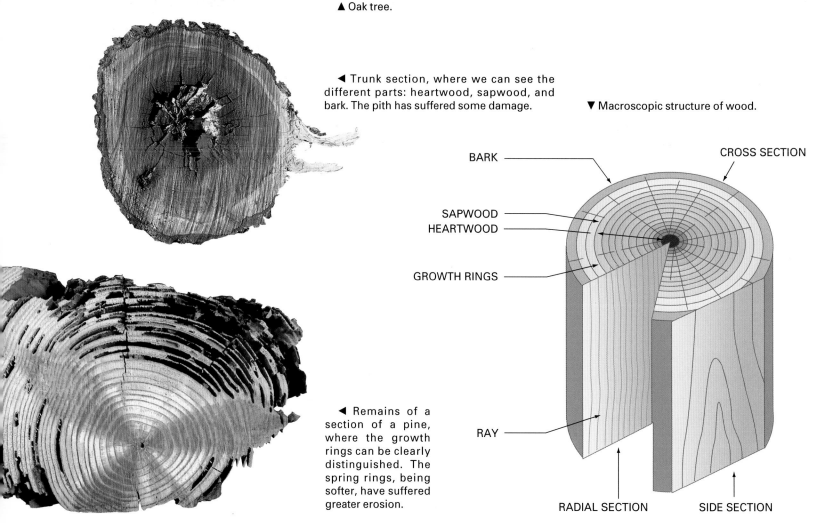

◀ Remains of a section of a pine, where the growth rings can be clearly distinguished. The spring rings, being softer, have suffered greater erosion.

BARK

CROSS SECTION

SAPWOOD

HEARTWOOD

GROWTH RINGS

RAY

RADIAL SECTION

SIDE SECTION

Biodeterioration can be defined as the combination of damage, wear, and changes produced by biological agents in organic material. In wood, the biological agents responsible for deterioration are microorganisms (especially fungi) as well as more specialized organisms (insects).

Microorganisms

The greater the humidity, the more susceptible wood is to the action of fungi. Like all organic material, wood is—to a greater or lesser degree—hygroscopic, which is to say, its relative humidity tends to be the same as the humidity in its surroundings. Various studies have shown that wood with a 20% humidity level is vulnerable to fungi, and a 30% humidity level—its saturation point—is the optimum environment for fungi to develop. Sugars and starches, as well as some components of the cellular walls, constitute the main source of nutrients for fungi. Fungi can develop on the wood's surface or in the cracks in conditions that promote deterioration: high relative humidity, poor ventilation, direct contact with the ground, and so on. This would be the case of wood objects from archaeological excavations or underwater sites. Some types of fungi can cause relatively extensive stains on the wood either by freeing pigments or through their own colonizing action, but in either case their effect on the wood itself is minimal compared to that of the fungi previously mentioned, which can destroy the walls that form the cells.

Some airborne bacteria can degrade the structural elements of wood or promote infestation by other microorganisms, since their action increases its permeability.

Wood Borers

It is insects, however, that are responsible for the greatest damage to wood. Wood-boring insects not only eat wood, but they live, develop, and reproduce in the wood.

As in the case of fungi, the sugars and starches are the main food source of wood-boring insects. Some species, however, eat partially decomposed cellulose, some eat all of these substances indiscriminately, and others only certain kinds of wood. There are also species that consume different elements at different stages in their life cycle. The life cycle consists of four phases: egg, larva, pupa, and adult (this last stage is arrived at after several mutations). The processes of mutation take place throughout the life of the insects until adulthood, since they have exoskeletons that have to be shed as they grow and complete their life cycle. Like all animals, insects absorb oxygen and release carbon dioxide, breathing through a system of tubes (tracheae) connected to exterior air holes. They cannot regulate their body temperature, however, which is why their growth, maturation, and reproduction take place only at certain temperatures. They slow down as the temperature drops, and

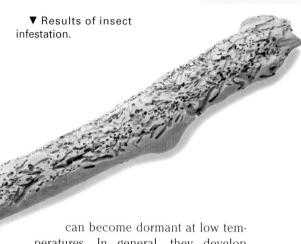

▼ Results of insect infestation.

can become dormant at low temperatures. In general, they develop quickly at around 75°F (25°C), slow their activity between 60 and 75°F (15 and 25°C) and stop breathing at temperatures below 50°F (10°C).

In order to measure the magnitude of the problem that wood borers represent for any wood object, it is important to understand their method of attack, especially if we keep in mind that the hole that signals their presence is produced by an adult that is likely to colonize other wood objects or pieces. The female lays her eggs in any crevice, crack or hole in the wood. Weeks later the larva emerges and immediately penetrates the wood, where it will live during the larval stage. It will change into a pupa, boring numerous tunnels throughout this period. Once it reaches the adult stage, after another mutation, the insect will bore its final tunnel to leave the wood. It will then fly to another piece of wood to lay its eggs.

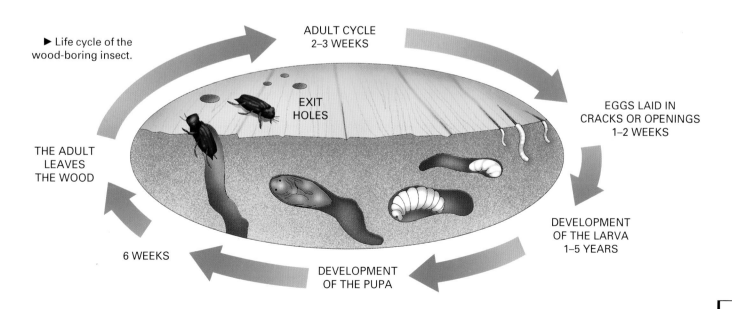

▶ Life cycle of the wood-boring insect.

ADULT CYCLE
2–3 WEEKS

EXIT HOLES

THE ADULT LEAVES THE WOOD

EGGS LAID IN CRACKS OR OPENINGS
1–2 WEEKS

6 WEEKS

DEVELOPMENT OF THE PUPA

DEVELOPMENT OF THE LARVA
1–5 YEARS

Identifying Wood Borers

There are different kinds of insects that can attack wood. Here we will point out only the most important ones:

Anobium punctatum. Wood Beetle

The wood beetle is the most widespread species of wood borer. These insects find ideal conditions for their development in countries with temperate climates, since they require mild temperatures and high relative humidity. Adults leave a characteristic trail of sawdust or wood powder near holes.

Xestobium rufovillosum

This species prefers to attack woods like walnut or elm.

Hylotrupes bajulus

This species, with a preference for conifers, has become a great menace in some countries with temperate climates. Wood severely attacked by these insects re-mains intact on the surface, while the interior can be completely destroyed. For this reason, it is difficult to detect infestation. These insects can become a serious problem in buildings constructed entirely of wood or with wooden structural elements like beams.

Nacerdes melanura

This species can develop in wood that is in contact with water.

Parasitic Wasps

Some species of parasitic wasps are found in wood that has been attacked by wood beetles. These wasps lay their eggs in the larva of the *Anobium* and develop along with the host larva. Once they reach their adult phase, they exit the wood through a different, smaller hole than the beetle.

Termites

Termites (a name that covers different species of the order *Isoptera*) are social insects (like bees) that live in colonies with a complex structure, consisting of different classes or castes—workers, soldiers, king and queen—together with eggs and larvae. Termites can live either in dry wood or wet wood that has begun to decompose, and there are also subterranean species. An infestation of termites often represents a serious problem for the wood structures because termites leave the surface of the wood intact and, therefore, are difficult to detect.

Mode of Entry

Wood borers do not appear spontaneously in wood. Their mode of entry is obvious: contact with another infested wood object (where there is still activity), as well as through doors, windows, grills, and ventilation systems. They are sometimes difficult to detect, because several years can pass from the time of attack until the adult leaves the wood. An attack may be indicated by the appearance of new holes in the wood, by the

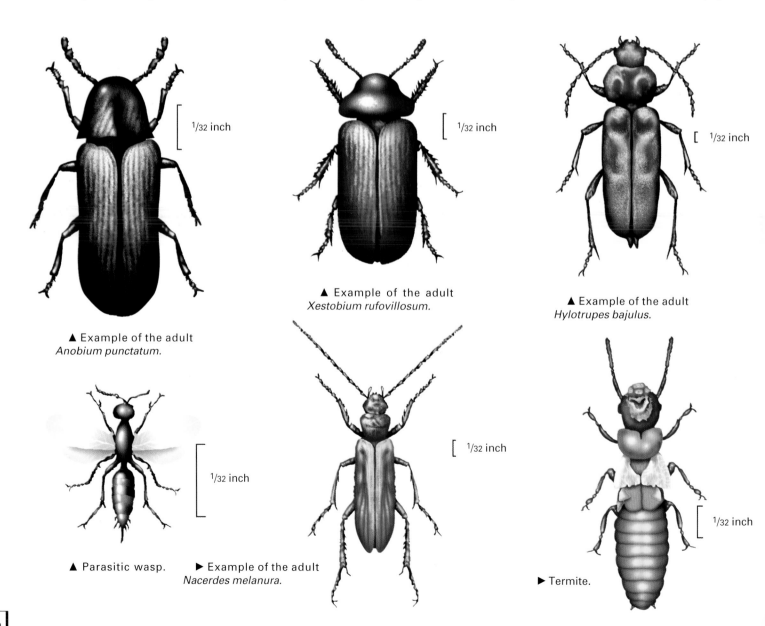

1/32 inch

▲ Example of the adult
Anobium punctatum.

1/32 inch

▲ Example of the adult
Xestobium rufovillosum.

1/32 inch

▲ Example of the adult
Hylotrupes bajulus.

1/32 inch

▲ Parasitic wasp.   ▶ Example of the adult
Nacerdes melanura.

1/32 inch

1/32 inch

▶ Termite.

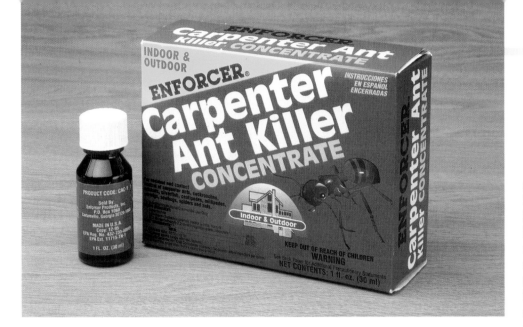

characteristic sawdust or powder, as well as by the presence of adults flying in the immediate area. In the case of furniture, attacks can occur in areas that are not visible or easily accessible: the back or bottom of the piece, the insides of drawers, and so on. In the structural elements of wood buildings, attacks can occur in both upper and lower floors (birds and other animals are very often carriers of these insects).

Traps are a help in detecting attacks, but never a way to eliminate the problem. They are based on the simple system of attracting an adult into an enclosure where he will become stuck to a strong adhesive. The insects are attracted by a material that releases pheromones (a substance that causes a sexual attraction) in the interior of the enclosure. The ideal time for placing traps is from the beginning of spring until the beginning of autumn, because the adult insects emerge when the required temperature is reached. Therefore, if the temperature is ideal all year (whether from climate or indoor heating systems), it will be necessary to maintain traps year-round, replacing them as indicated by the manufacturer. It is not recommended that traps be stored for a long time, because some have expiration dates.

Methods of Elimination

Systems for eliminating wood borers can be just curative (killing insects) or also preventive (avoiding future attacks), the latter being preferable. The many methods of elimination can be divided into two groups based on whether they are physical or chemical.

Physical Methods

These methods involve modifying environmental conditions to kill the insects, a simple curative action. They usually require special techniques and can only be employed by laboratories or by specialized companies and in large institutions. Freezing, gamma rays, and transforming the atmosphere where the insects live have all been employed. This last technique consists of eliminating the oxygen in the medium where the insects are developing, killing them in all phases of their life cycle by asphyxiation. This technique does no harm to the environment and is completely safe for humans.

Chemical Methods

These methods involve killing wood borers by applying toxic substances (poisons). It is important to keep in mind that some of the substances can, depending on the ingredients and the concentration, be harmful to people and the environment. Gases and liquids are used. The use of gases almost always requires special

▲ A spray insecticide against several types of insects.

gas chambers, which have safety systems (filters, safety valves, and so on) and are operated by expert personnel. Different gases have been used, some of them now prohibited in many countries as being cancer causing. One compound, paradichlorobenzine, comes in solid form, although its killing action is caused by the vapors it emanates; it is used in high concentrations, which can be toxic for humans. The efficacy of methods based on the use of gases ends once the application is over; therefore, their effect is only curative. On the other hand, liquid insecticides containing substances that act against wood borers are diluted in solvents to enhance penetrability. Success depends on how well a solution penetrates the area that has suffered attack. The effect of a liquid insecticide is curative as well as preventive: If it has completely penetrated the wood its efficiency can be lasting and will prevent new attacks. Some of the substances used are lindens, permetrines, and piretrines. The first two can be toxic if they are present in large concentrations or if they are applied in places that are not well ventilated. It is a good idea to always use a respirator during application. Piretrines are substances extracted from tropical flowers, which seem to contain lower levels of toxicity, although there have been reports of noxious effects in certain animals. Certain substances of vegetable origin are now being studied with an eye to developing liquid insecticides that are less toxic for humans and that have little or no impact on the environment by eliminating residues and cumulative effects.

◀ Example of a preventive product for controlling insects.

Environmental Causes and Conservation

Humidity and Temperature

As has been previously pointed out, temperature and humidity are two related factors whose effects are combined. In fact, humidity is the greatest cause of physical deterioration of organic material in general and wood in particular.

Air always contains water vapor, that is, humidity. The capacity of the air to hold water vapor varies according to the temperature: the higher the temperature, the greater its capacity. One cubic yard (1 m) of air at 85°F (30°C) can hold up to 1 oz. (30 g) of water vapor; the same amount of air at 68°F (20°C) can hold up to 1/2 oz. (17 g) of water vapor, at 50°F (10°C) up to 5/16 oz. (9 g), and at 40°F (5°C) up to 1/4 oz. (7 g). These are the so-called saturation points at which the air can hold no more water vapor. If the quantity is exceeded or the temperature drops, the water condenses into a liquid state.

To quantify the humidity of the air around us, the concept of relative humidity is applied: a relation expressed as a percentage of real water vapor in the air and how much there could be if the air was saturated. The values vary from 0 to 100%. Relative humidity fluctuates with changes in temperature.

Most organic materials contain a greater or lesser quantity of water vapor. All animals and vegetables are partly composed of water; when we transform them, they dry out and their cells lose water, but they still have the ability to contain it again. Because of this, all

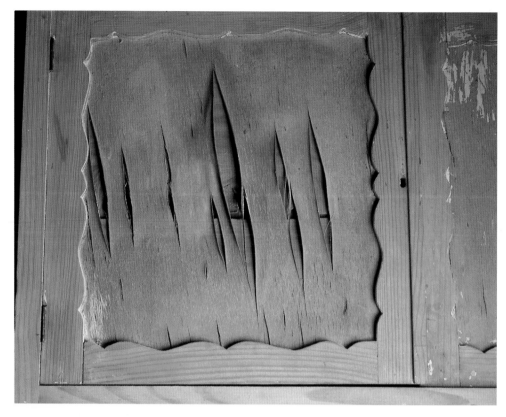

▲ The consequences of variations in humidity and temperature.

organic material establishes a dynamic balance according to the relative humidity of its surroundings. If the water content of the surroundings increases, the object will tend to absorb water from the surroundings; if, on the contrary, the water content of the surroundings decreases, the object will tend to release water into the surroundings.

Wood usually has between 12 and 20% water content by weight, and the larger its surface area and the thinner the wood, the more rapidly the water content can change.

Excessive temperatures provoke chemical reactions in the cellulose contained in the wood. In general, for every 18°F (10°C) that the temperature increases, the chemical reactions that have already begun in the organic material double.

A RAPID CHANGE IN RELATIVE HUMIDITY FROM 50 TO 100%

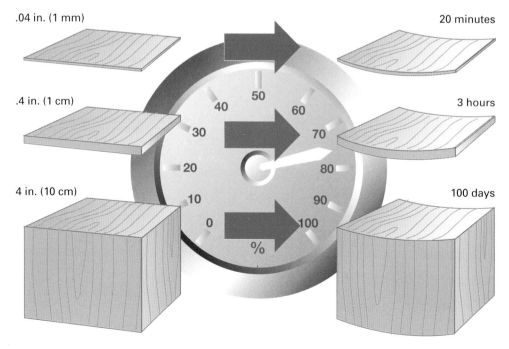

.04 in. (1 mm)　　　　20 minutes

.4 in. (1 cm)　　　　3 hours

4 in. (10 cm)　　　　100 days

◀ Diagram of the reaction of different thicknesses of wood of a standard density to changes in relative humidity.

▲ Diagram of electromagnetic radiation.

Light

Light is the part of electromagnetic radiation that can be perceived by the human eye. Electromagnetic radiation exists as waves: the shorter the longitude, the more potential energy, which is more pernicious. The wavelengths range from those used by radio and television (the longest) to x-rays and gamma rays (the shortest), with the visible spectrum located between infrared and ultraviolet.

Infrared and ultraviolet rays cause the harmful effects of radiation on organic material, including wood. Infrared rays cause the wood's temperature to rise, resulting in shrinkage. Ultraviolet rays promote oxidation in the wood, changing its color and physical properties. It is important to keep in mind that sunlight is composed of great quantities of infrared rays, visible light, and ultraviolet rays. Incandescent and halogen bulbs emit large quantities of infrared rays (which cause heating) and visible light. Fluorescent tubes do not emit infrared rays, only visible light and ultraviolet rays.

The harmful effect is produced in direct proportion to the time of exposure and the type of radiation. It is always cumulative and combines with other factors affecting deterioration.

Steps for Conserving Wood

As we have seen up to now, many factors and conditions can provoke deterioration in wood. Nevertheless, certain practices help prevent, stop or limit this deterioration, thus conserving the wood.

Waxes and varnishes not only beautify wood but also act as protection against wood borers and brusque changes in relative humidity. They help minimize changes in the wood and keep it

from losing too much moisture. Wood borers tend to lay their eggs in cracks or holes in the wood; if they are faced with a polished surface, their attack will be more difficult.

To locate insect infestations in wood furniture it is good to periodically inspect the backs and undersides, because these usually have lower quality finishes and are more prone to attack. Insect activity decreases at lower temperatures, so it is not advisable to raise the temperature excessively during the winter months. Furniture made of wood fiberboard or medium density fiberboard (MDF)

does not suffer from wood borer attacks, because adhesives used in their manufacture contain insect repellent.

It is of utmost importance to keep furniture clean, since accumulated dust can increase the relative humidity on the surface of the wood by up to 10%. High humidity levels can produce fungi, warp veneer, and so on.

Installing heavy cotton or linen curtains in windows and balconies can minimize the effects of ultraviolet rays. These common materials can filter out a large part of the radiation.

◀ Insect screen.

*I*t is impossible to cover all of the materials and products that can be used in restoring wood. Each restoration project will be unique and specific to a particular object (furniture, door, beam, and so on), and each will require the use of unique products and processes. Nevertheless, we can establish some general guidelines concerning products and materials, as well as tools and processes (which we will cover later). Choosing from among different materials and solutions, as well as various techniques, will depend on one's experience in the trade, which requires dedication and above all time.

When it comes to materials, the proper wood is of the utmost importance, and it can be found in different forms. Most commonly used materials have been manufactured for uses that are completely unrelated to restoration, but without these materials, it would be impossible to carry out any project. Various safety and protective materials are necessary for the restorer's health. Finally, there is a group of related materials that are used in fields like woodworking or shipping and that will be of great help in the work.

The products are presented in order of their use in the restoration process: poisons, cleaners, strippers, bleaches, adhesives, stains, and fillers. Products used for the final finishing of wood deserve a separate chapter of their own.

Materials

Wood

There are many classes and species of trees and bushes that are used for their wood. Their use varies considerably according to different zones and countries, and for this reason, we will only cover the most common ones. This listing of species and types is meant to help establish a basic knowledge of woods.

When one is faced with the task of restoring an object made of an unknown wood, the first step is to study its characteristics and behavior. This helps in determining a restoration method, the necessary processes, needed steps and the most suitable system for conserving the object.

◀ Birch. *Betula pendula, Betula alba, Betula verrucosa.*
Light colored, from yellowish to reddish, with a short, compact grain.

▼ Fir. *Abies alba.*
Light colored, with a long straight grain. Great difference between spring wood and autumn wood, with wide annual rings.

▲ Poplar. *Populus alba.*
A whitish yellow wood, also sometimes gray.

▶ Maple. *Acer campestre.*
Light colored, a fine, dense wood.

▼ Bird's Eye Maple. *Acer campestre.*
Owes its name to the characteristic pattern of knots.

▼ Boxwood. *Buxus sempervirens.*
Hard, dense, and even-grained wood, yellowish in color.

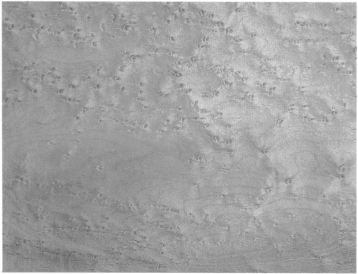

► Mahogany. *Swietenia.*
Characteristically dark red wood, with a curved and even grain that is dense and durable.

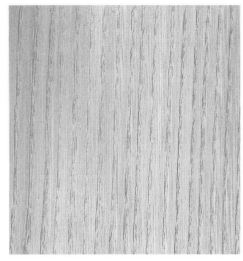

◄ Chestnut. *Castanea sativa.*
A reddish ochre colored wood with a coarse grain.

▼ Cedar. *Cedrus atlantica.*
A pinkish wood with irregular growth rings.

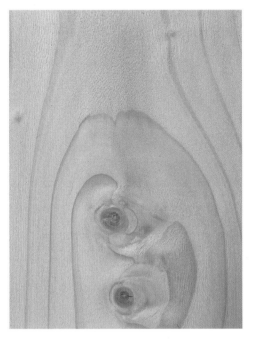

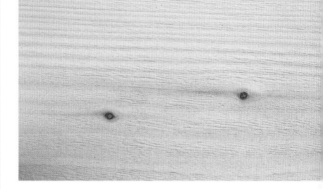

▲ Cypress. *Cypressus sempervirens.*
A light brown wood with a reddish grain.

◄ Cherry. *Prunus avium.*
A reddish brown wood with a straight grain.

▼ Ebony. *Diospyros.*
A very hard, fine-grained, and heavy wood. Deep black color.

▼ Ash. *Fraximus excelsior.*
A wood with a handsome grain and yellowish color.

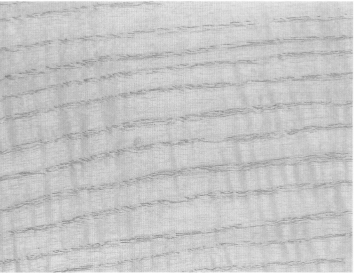

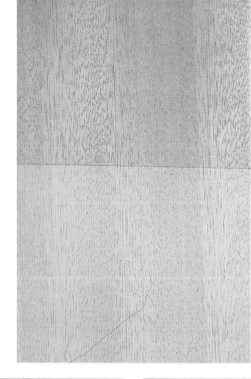

◀ Myrtle. *Fagara heitzii.*
A very light wood, similar to lemon.

▶ Beech. *Fagus sylvatica.*
A yellowish, even-grained wood with few knots.

▼ American Walnut. *Juglans nigra.*
A darker walnut than the European.

▲ Elm. *Ulmus.*
A dark red wood with a coarse grain.

▶ Walnut. *Juglans regia.*
A light brown wood with a characteristic wavy grain.

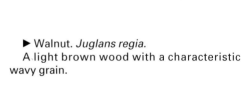

◀ Olive. *Olea europea.*
A yellowish wood with a dark grain, hard and compact.

▶ Palisander. *Machaerium. Dalbergia.*
Woods whose colors range from dark red to violet or almost black, some fine grained and others coarse.

▶ Pearwood. *Pirus comunis.*
A pinkish brown hardwood with a fine grain.

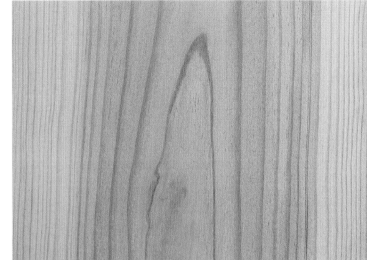

▼ Oregon Pine. *Pseudotsuga douglasii.*
A very resinous dark wood.

▲ Norway Spruce. *Picea abies.*
A whitish yellow wood with a dark grain.

▼ Yellow Pine. *Pinus palustris.*
Characterized by its red grain.

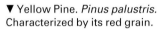

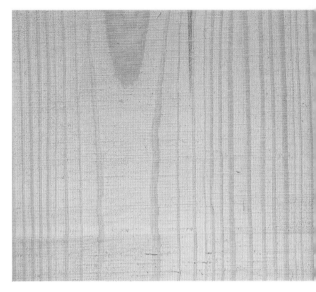

▲ Oak. *Quercus robur.*
A very hard and dense wood, straight grained with an earthy yellow color.

◀ Plantain. *Platanus orientalis. Platanus ecerifolia.*
A dark-toned wood with a pronounced iridescence, hard and heavy.

▶ Teakwood. *Tectona grandis.*
A very durable hardwood with a dark red color.

Wood Parts and Pieces

For convenience, you should keep a variety of wood pieces in the workshop to make the repairs that each piece of furniture requires. It is a good idea to save and store old wood, the bottoms of old drawers and wardrobes, veneers, legs from unusable chairs, and so on. In each case, the wood closest in color will be chosen, always respecting the direction of the grain as well as the original species. If the coloration is different, there are ways to stain it that can be used to even out the tone and hide the added parts.

The stock wood pieces that are used most often in the restoration workshop are solid wood boards, veneers, dowels, molding, and legs.

Boards

Wood boards are used to replace broken or rotten parts of furniture. It is a good idea to repair and clean the damaged area before joining the new part to it.

◀ Boards

Veneers

It is common to have to add pieces of veneer to furniture that is being restored. There are many wood species available in veneer form on the market, which greatly simplifies the job.

Dowels

Dowels are used to reinforce joints; the most useful are the grooved ones, because their greater surface area gives greater adherence than the smooth ones.

Quarter-round and half-round moldings of various widths are used to hold glass in doors. Various other profiles have many uses.

▶ Dowels and molding.

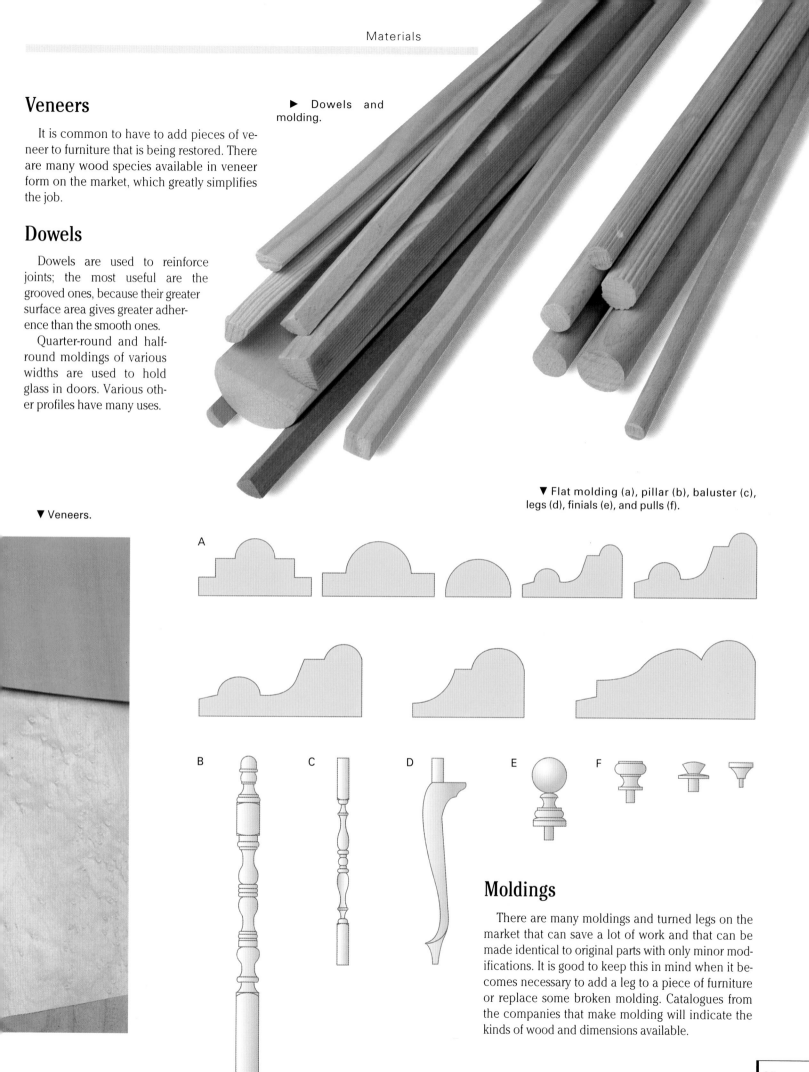

▼ Veneers.

▼ Flat molding (a), pillar (b), baluster (c), legs (d), finials (e), and pulls (f).

A

B   C   D   E   F

Moldings

There are many moldings and turned legs on the market that can save a lot of work and that can be made identical to original parts with only minor modifications. It is good to keep this in mind when it becomes necessary to add a leg to a piece of furniture or replace some broken molding. Catalogues from the companies that make molding will indicate the kinds of wood and dimensions available.

Commonly Used Materials and Safety Products

Basic Materials

▲ Rags.

◀ Steel wool.

There are some basic materials that are used in all restoration projects, regardless of the treatment that the furniture piece may require, that should always be kept on hand. Other supplies may not be so common, but it is a good idea to keep them in the workshop since they are used often.

Steel Wool

This is used to remove or to polish varnish. It is a good idea to have two kinds, a number 000 and a coarser one. They are sold in small packages or in rolls for industrial use.

Cotton Strands

Strands of cotton thread are used to apply products to the wood like strippers, wax, varnish, and so on. They adapt well to any surface and penetrate in hard-to-reach, inaccessible places. Cotton strands are sold by the bag. Cheesecloth may be substituted if you are unable to find these.

Sandpaper

The secret to a good finish is good sanding, and several papers of various grits are necessary for each project. The number range of grits used starts at 80 and goes to 320, and it is advisable to have six different grits on hand.

▲ Various sandpapers.

▼ Cotton strands.

▼ Syringes.

▼ Brushes.

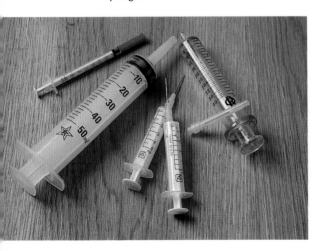

▲ Safety glasses.

▲▼ Masks and respirators.

Rags

Preferably, rags should be of lint-free cotton. They are used for polishing, cleaning furniture, cleaning metals, for polishing pads, and so on. Finely woven used cotton rags are best for making pads for French polishing.

Syringes

These are very useful for applying insecticides, injecting white glue into hard to reach joints, filling wood, and so on. It is good to keep a variety of sizes to meet your different needs.

Brushes

All types are needed, including sable hair and very fine brushes. They are used to apply all kinds of products to wood, as well as for finishing and retouching jobs.

Safety Equipment Products

Although the sense of touch is necessary for detecting a good finish, or even for checking the results of sanding, it is sometimes necessary to wear neoprene gloves. They should be used with abrasive or corrosive products to avoid direct contact with the skin.

Safety glasses are highly recommended for certain stripping techniques and when polishing metal.

Respirators with specific filters are used to avoid breathing toxic vapors and masks are worn to keep from inhaling solid materials.

Hearing protection is advisable when you are using machines that generate a lot of noise.

▲ Gloves.

▼ Hearing protectors.

RESPIRATOR AND FILTER CHART		
COLOR	TYPE	USE
	A	Organic vapors.
	AP	Organic vapors + dust.
	B	Inorganic acid gases.
	BP	Inorganic acid gases + smoke and fumes.
	E	Sulfuric acid.
	EP	Sulfuric acid + dust, smoke, and fumes.
	K	Ammonia.
	KP	Ammonia + dust, smoke, and fumes.
	AB	Organic vapors + inorganic acid gases.
	ABP	Organic vapors + dust, smoke, and fumes.
	P	Dust, smoke, and fumes.
	ABEK	All purpose filter for gases.
	ABEP	All purpose filter for gases + dust, smoke, and fumes.
	ABEKP	All purpose filter for gases + dust, smoke, and fumes.

Products

▲ Insecticides.

Insecticides

Treatments for insect infestation should always be applied whenever there is an indication of the presence of insects, even if there are no signs of activity. These treatments come in liquid form, and must be injected into the holes left by insects. There are reliable, environmentally friendly products that are harmless to humans and the environment; these are more highly recommended than those that abound on the market, which generally are quite toxic.

▲ Products for marble.

▲ Degreasing mixtures and soap paste.

For Cleaning

Sometimes abandoned furniture is rescued from the attic or is bought at a flea market. These pieces require a thorough cleaning more than restoration. Antique furniture in homes can collect dust, soot, and pollution over the years and also need cleaning.

This cleaning will not damage the varnish but just remove the grime that covers the furniture piece and bring back its original shine.

A degreasing mixture (neutral soap, water, and ammonia) or a soap paste made of neutral soap flakes mixed with wax can be used.

Metal furniture hardware, often quite tarnished, should be cleaned very well, since it highlights the furniture. The best way is to remove the parts for polishing to avoid damaging the wood. The screws and nails are often rusted, and they should be left to soak for a few minutes in any commercially available product sold for this purpose. After keyholes, pulls, hinges, and so on are removed, they should be cleaned and polished.

Marble tops should be cleaned without being polished, because they would lose their characteristic patina. There are products on the market that do a very good job. A final application of a good furniture wax, followed by hand polishing, will result in an excellent finish.

▼ Products for metals.

Solvents

Solvents are chemicals that are used to remove varnish or painted finishes on furniture.

Ethyl alcohol is a good solvent for old varnish. It has to be applied liberally on a small area to be able to remove the varnish from that spot. It is recommended because it is harmless and works well.

Turpentine or paint thinner can be used to remove nitrocellulose-based varnish or wax, but a respirator should be used with thinner, because it is toxic if inhaled.

When alcohol does not work, other solvents can be used. They are generically known as strippers, and can be used to remove either varnish or paint. These are chemicals that should be handled with caution and always with gloves. If they come in contact with skin, flush thoroughly with water. Be sure to follow the manufacturers' instructions. Strippers can generally be used with any variety of wood.

Caustic soda diluted in water can be used for stripping solid pine furniture. The concentration can be adjusted according to the thickness of the paint and the quality of the wood.

Bleaches

Bleaches are used to remove any paint or wood stains that remain trapped in the pores after stripping. Commercially available products are based on oxalic acid dissolved in water and are sometimes mixed with other additives. After drying the item, the crystallized acid should be flushed with water until it is totally eliminated.

A supersaturated solution can be mixed with this acid and water by placing enough crystals in warm water so that some undissolved acid always remains in the bottom of the container.

Hydrogen peroxide is a very popular bleach (at 30% concentration). It should be neutralized with water after getting the desired color.

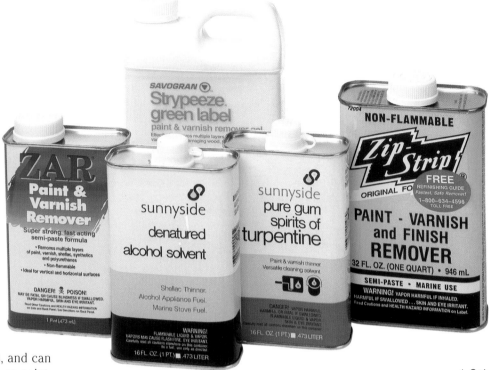

Adhesives

White carpenter's glue is the most commonly used adhesive. It is a polyvinyl acetate and is water soluble. Sold ready to use, it is used for all types of restoration work. The excess glue that often seeps out of the joints can be removed with a wet rag. A safe drying time for a good bond is 24 hours.

A cyanoacrylate-based adhesive can be used for small joints or spots that are not subject to a lot of pressure. It is resistant and very effective, but it is very dangerous.

Hot-melt glue sticks that are applied with a special electric glue gun give good results; they are used when clamps will not fit or when a fast-drying glue is necessary.

Animal glues, like rabbit-skin glue or fish glue, are not often used because it is difficult to keep them hot.

▲ Solvents.

▼ Bleaches.

▶ Adhesives.

Stains

After being stripped, a piece of furniture can still have stains, differences in color between different kinds of wood, partial aging if it has been exposed to light unevenly, recent additions, and so on. To remedy all this, and to achieve uniformity in color, we often recommend the use of stains.

Stains are also used to create certain colors in furniture, different from the wood used in its manufacture. The easiest stains to apply are water-based aniline dyes, although they have the drawback of raising the grain of the wood. They must be sanded before they dry.

These are prepared by dissolving the dye in water, and a wide range of colors can be obtained by adding color pigments in powder or liquid form. Using hot water and shaking well helps to mix the colors thoroughly. The solutions will last a long time if a few drops of bleach are added to discourage the growth of bacteria.

Alcohol-based aniline dyes are more appropriate for today's woods, because they are less porous and because of the variety of colors that are available on the market. The difficulty in using them on antique furniture comes from the quick evaporation of the alcohol,

◀ Stains.

which causes brush marks and streaking, making it difficult to achieve a uniform finish.

Other chemical dyes, such as potassium dichromate, tannic acid, or iron sulfide, should be used with caution, avoiding contact with skin, because they can be toxic. Aniline dyes are recommended because they are less toxic and dangerous and because of their good results.

Asphaltum can be used to age new wood used on furniture bottoms, drawers, and parts that will not be treated with shellac or varnish but need to match the rest of the piece. It can be diluted with alcohol or turpentine to lighten its tone.

▼ Fillers.

Fillers

Pastes and waxes are used to fill small areas where the wood has disappeared, whether from breakage, aging, bumps, or wood borers. We will use different materials according to the surface that needs to be treated.

To fill holes and channels left by wood borers, hard waxes can be used. They are available on the market in bar form in a number of colors. Before application, it is a good idea to wet the wood with alcohol to see what its color will be when it is varnished, and then choose a wax that is the exact same tone. To apply, soften the wax and work it with your hands; using a wood spatula, press the wax to cause it to penetrate the holes.

When a larger surface needs repair, tinted waxes can be used. They are solid at room temperature but liquid when warmed in a double boiler, since their base is beeswax and paraffin. This wax is applied with a spatula, and the excess scraped off. It should be tinted before application to give it a close enough tone so it will not be noticed.

There are synthetic fillers on the market, one-part or two-part products that can be stained after they dry. These fillers are also applied with a spatula, and are very useful for small touch-up tasks. They can be carved with gouges and chisels to give them any shape. Synthetic fillers are expensive, however, and therefore not usually used for restoration work.

Fabrics, Tapes, and Paper Tape

When it is necessary to protect surfaces from getting scratched or stained, masking tape is used. It is good to have various widths for use with different projects. When transporting furniture that has been restored, paper tape can be used to hold the furniture blankets covering the piece to prevent damage.

Boards in the backs of wardrobes or in drawers that have separated as a result of changes in humidity can be covered with paper tape or fabric on the back or underside. This way light will not show through the cracks.

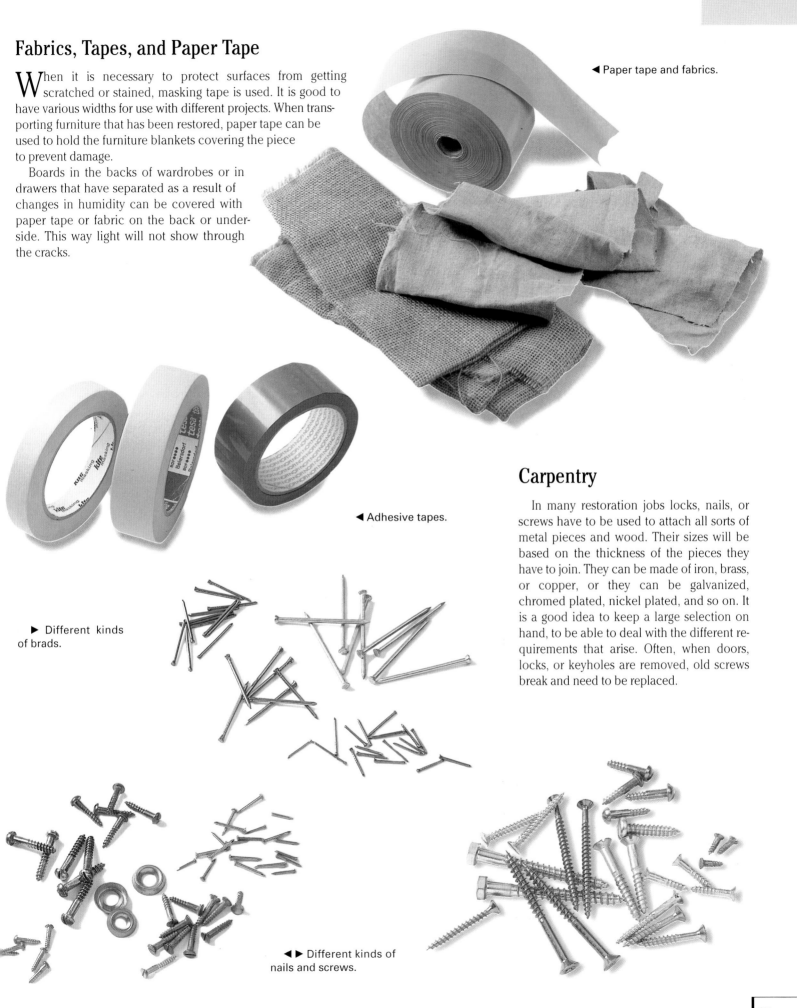

◀ Paper tape and fabrics.

◀ Adhesive tapes.

▶ Different kinds of brads.

Carpentry

In many restoration jobs locks, nails, or screws have to be used to attach all sorts of metal pieces and wood. Their sizes will be based on the thickness of the pieces they have to join. They can be made of iron, brass, or copper, or they can be galvanized, chromed plated, nickel plated, and so on. It is a good idea to keep a large selection on hand, to be able to deal with the different requirements that arise. Often, when doors, locks, or keyholes are removed, old screws break and need to be replaced.

◀ ▶ Different kinds of nails and screws.

Finishes

The finish on a piece of furniture is the result of the processes designed to achieve the final desired appearance. Sometimes this takes several steps and many products.

Furniture Wax

Furniture wax is a mixture of animal, vegetable, and/or mineral wax that, together with a solvent, makes up a solid that feels tacky to the touch. There are many kinds of furniture waxes on the market, but only the paste form is used in restoration. The base of this product is pure beeswax combined with turpentine and paraffin, along with other waxes and additives that give it specific properties, like hardness, color, odor, or gloss. It imparts a satin finish to the wood.

Hard Waxes

Hard waxes come in bar form and a large selection of colors that can be adapted to any shade of wood. They are used to fill small defects and, above all, to cover holes left by insects.

Varnish

In traditional furniture a nitrocellulose varnish is used, which fills the pores of the wood and imparts a glossy or a satin finish to the surface, depending on the type of varnish used. It is toxic, so a respirator should be used during application. The layer of varnish is not very hard, and it scratches easily. It can be diluted with thinner.

Other more desirable varnishes like polyurethane are more recent inventions, and are not appropriate for period furniture.

▼ ▲ Different types of waxes. Homemade (above) and different kinds of commercial waxes (below): colorless, tinted, and powder form.

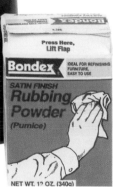

▼ Different hard waxes. There are many colors for matching restored wood, and different sizes and consistencies for easy use.

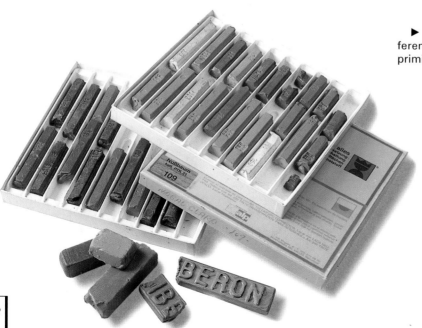

▶ Varnishes of different weights for priming or final finish.

◀ Shellac.

▶ Ingredients for the French polish paste.

French Polish

This technique requires very finely ground pumice stone, liquid Vaseline, and alcohol. A paste is formed with these ingredients, which fills the pores of the wood and prepares it for a high quality glossy finish. This paste is applied by hand with a pad, applying pressure and wiping the surface of the wood with a circular motion.

▲ Types of shellac in flake form.

▼ Touch-up pens and stains.

Shellac

Shellac is the only resin of animal rather than vegetable origin. It is the secretion of the lac beetle, which lives in different types of trees in India and Thailand. It is available in flakes and is soluble in alcohol.

Shellac forms a glossy film that is hard and elastic when dry. It ages with time, turning yellow, and is vulnerable to water. A shellac finish is of high quality but very delicate.

Retouching Pens and Stains

For minor retouching, even on varnish, numerous pens are available in all of the colors of the woods that are most commonly used in furniture manufacturing.

Alcohol based stains can be very useful. They will not raise the grain and are resistant to light. They are usually applied with a sable brush, and are blended before the alcohol evaporates to hide the repair.

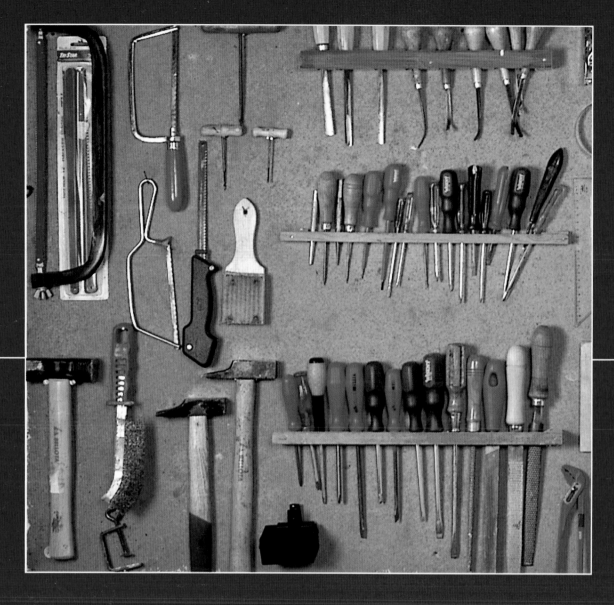

Tools

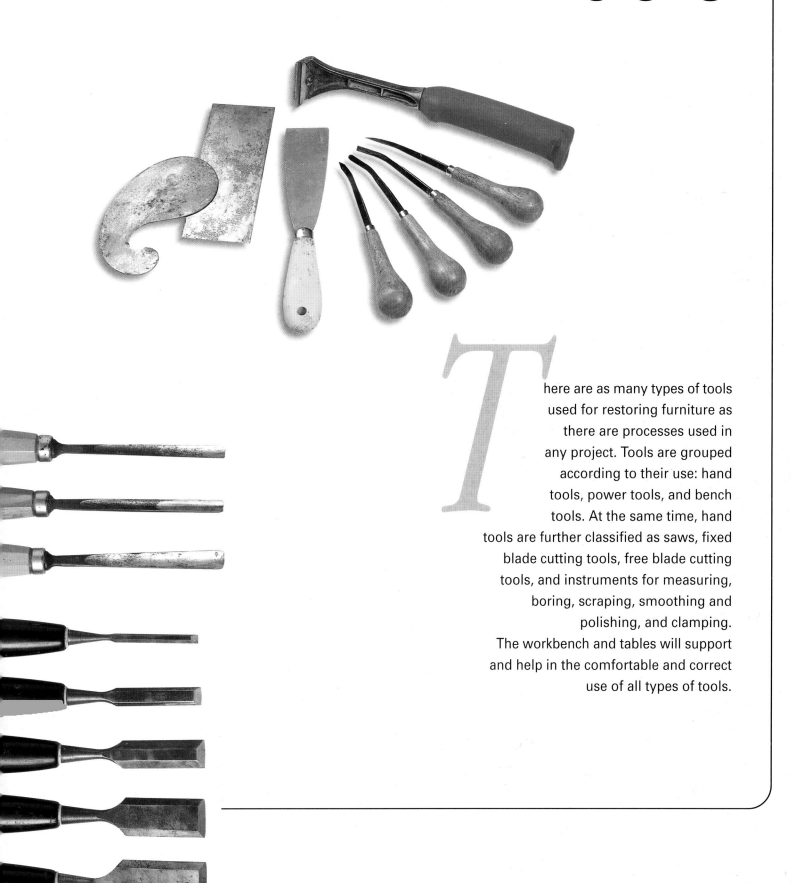

There are as many types of tools used for restoring furniture as there are processes used in any project. Tools are grouped according to their use: hand tools, power tools, and bench tools. At the same time, hand tools are further classified as saws, fixed blade cutting tools, free blade cutting tools, and instruments for measuring, boring, scraping, smoothing and polishing, and clamping. The workbench and tables will support and help in the comfortable and correct use of all types of tools.

Hand Tools

Saws

Handsaw
Consists of a tapered blade that is very wide and strong, without a back, about $1/16$ inch (1 to 2 mm) thick. It is rigid, so it will not buckle while being used.

Backsaw
Used for fine, precision cuts. Its name comes from the reinforcing metal strip on the top edge of the blade.

Dovetail Saw
Similar to the backsaw, but smaller. It is used for very precise work.

Veneer Saw
Consists of a blade about $1/16$ inch (1 to 2 mm) thick and 3 to 4 inches (7 to 10 cm) long. It has teeth on both sides. Besides cutting veneer, it can be used for cutting dowels.

Hacksaw
Consists of a very narrow blade mounted in a metal frame. It is used for cutting metal.

Scroll Saw
Mainly used for marquetry or for small pieces of wood with curved forms. It consists of a very fine blade mounted vertically into a metal frame. The frames can be of different sizes. The blade should be mounted so that it always cuts on the pull.

Fixed Blade Cutting Tools

Block Plane
Consists of a wood block 8 to 12 inches (20 to 30 cm) long with a more or less slanted opening for inserting a blade held with a wedge. Used for smoothing and polishing wood.

Metal Plane
Used much like a block plane. It requires more technical skill than a wooden one, but it allows greater precision.

Jack Plane
Plane 20 to 30 inches (50 to 80 cm) long and 2 to 3 inches (5 to 8 cm) wide. It has a double blade and a handle, and is used to smooth wood surfaces.

Rabbet Plane
A narrow plane, about 1 inch (2 to 3 cm) wide. Its base is the same width as the blade.

▲ Handsaw (A), backsaw (B), dovetail saw (C), veneer saw (D), hacksaw, (E), and scroll saw (F).

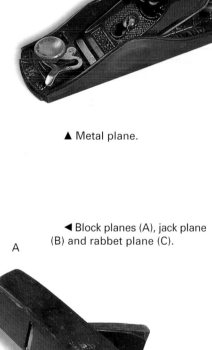

▲ Metal plane.

◄ Block planes (A), jack plane (B) and rabbet plane (C).

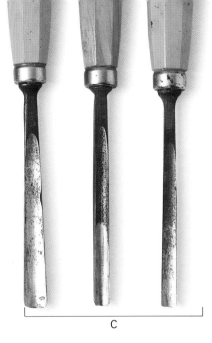

◄ Chisels (A), mortise chisel (B), and gouges (C).

B

A

C

Tools with Cutting Blades

Chisel

Composed of a steel blade with a horizontal cutting edge and a handle that is usually made of wood. Its width varies from $1/8$ inch to $1^1/2$ inches (4 to 40 mm). Used for making hollow cavities.

Mortise Chisel

A chisel with a thicker blade. Its width varies from $3/32$ inch to $3/4$ inch (2 to 20 mm) while its thickness increases in the same proportion. Used for cutting rectangular holes.

Gouge

Similar to a chisel, although the blade is curved and hollowed and it has different profiles.

Tools for Measuring, Marking, and Checking

Rulers

Used for measuring. There are different types made of wood, plastic, aluminum, or rolled metal tapes inside plastic or metal containers.

Straight Edge

A wood strip with straight edges that is used to draw straight lines and for checking flat surfaces. It can be of wood or metal, the latter being better because of its durability.

Try Square

Consists of two pieces of different lengths set at right angles. It is used to check the accuracy of right angles.

Sliding Bevel

Consists of two straight edges, one with a fixed screw, around which the other slides and rotates. Used to mark and check angles.

Marking Gauge

A wood instrument used to mark parallel lines on wood surfaces for cutting them to a desired size.

Dividers

Usually made of steel. Used to mark curves or to measure distances.

Calipers

Consists of a graduated ruler and a right angle at one end, where another graduated square slides. Used for precision measurements.

▼ Measuring devices (A), metal ruler (B), square (C), sliding bevel (D), marking gauge (E), compass (F), profile gauge (G), caliper (H), and level (I).

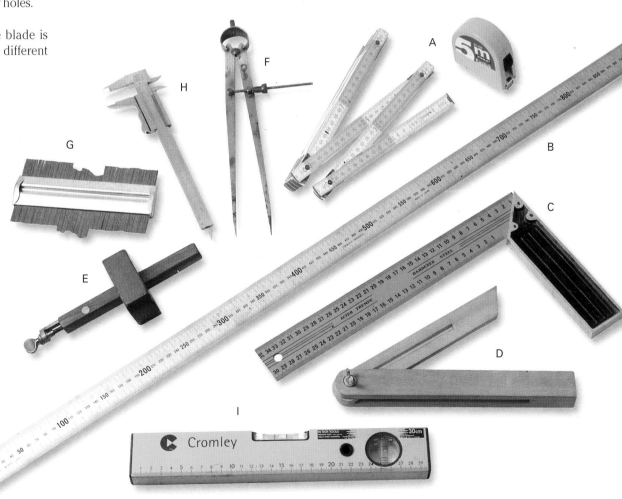

Tools for Striking and Pulling

Hammer
Steel head and wood handle. Used for driving nails and all striking tasks that cannot be done with the sole force of the hand.

Veneer Hammer
With a handle about 10 inches (25 cm) long and a head about 6 inches (15 cm) wide, it is an indispensable tool for veneering. It is used to squeeze excess glue toward the edges and to achieve complete adhesion between the veneer and the base.

Mallet
A hammer with a wooden head. Used for striking the handles of chisels and gouges, and for such things as joints and assemblies.

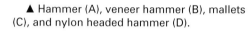

▲ Hammer (A), veneer hammer (B), mallets (C), and nylon headed hammer (D).

Hammer with Nylon Head
Used for nailing delicate pieces, like keyholes and pulls. The nylon head will not leave a mark on metal parts or wood.

▼ Pincers (A), pliers (B), nail sets (C), and nail puller (D).

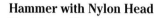

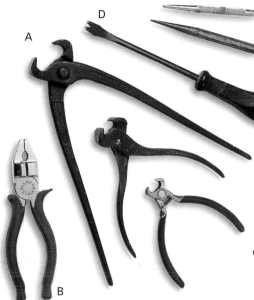

Pincers
Made of two steel parts attached with a bolt. Used for pulling nails or cutting.

Pliers
Made of steel with square or conical points. Used for cutting or twisting hard wire and similar materials.

Nail Set
Steel conical cylinder with a flattened point. Used to sink nail heads and brads.

Nail Puller
Steel bar with a handle at one end and a claw at the other. Used to grab the heads of nails and pull them.

Screwdriver
Made of a steel rod with one end corresponding to a particular kind of screw head, and a handle of plastic or wood at the other. There are many types and sizes. Used to drive and remove screws.

▲ Screwdrivers.

▼ Gimlets (A, B), awls (C), and hand drill (D).

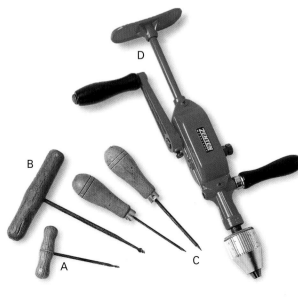

Tools for Boring Holes

Gimlet
Used to bore shallow holes and pre-drill holes for screws. It has a pointed end with threads and a handle for turning by hand. Larger ones can be turned using both hands.

Awl
It has a very fine metal point with a wood handle. Used for making small shallow holes.

Hand Drill
Drill with a chuck at one end, provided with a crank and a fixed pad for holding it in place. Allows rapid drilling.

▼ Rasps (A) and files (B).

Tools for Scraping, Smoothing, and Polishing

Rasps and Files

Made of tempered steel, these tools have teeth that remove small slivers of wood. They can have different cuts (coarse, bastard, and smooth) and shapes (square, flat, half-round, and so on). Rasps have coarse, triangular teeth; files have a grooved surface.

File Cleaner

A brush with short bristles, used to clean files and rasps.

Scraper Blades

Tempered steel blades that are flexible and of good quality. They are generally rectangular, although there are different shapes for fitting different surfaces. Their cutting action is produced by the burr on the edges.

Handled Scraper

A blade with a handle used for large areas and heavy work.

Gravers

Gravers have a blade that is pointed at one end and a wood handle. Used to scrape in corners where larger tools cannot reach, polish wood, or remove varnish. The points have different shapes.

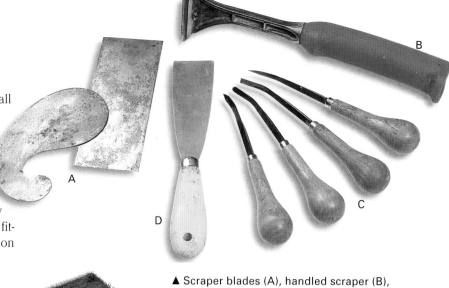

▲ Scraper blades (A), handled scraper (B), gravers (C), and paint scraper (D).

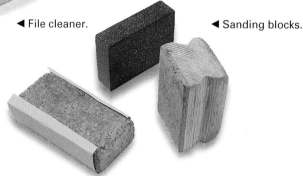

◀ File cleaner.

◀ Sanding blocks.

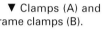

▼ Clamps (A) and frame clamps (B).

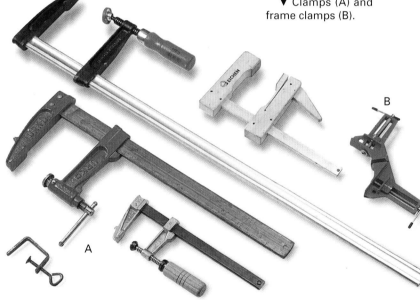

Four-Way Frame Clamp

Made of an adjustable band that surrounds the frame that is to be glued and a screw that is used to apply pressure.

Ring Clamps

Made of heavy steel wire. The elasticity of the material permits its use with small pieces.

Twine

Used for tying pieces together and for tourniquets.

▼ Spring clamps (A), twine (B), ring clamps (C), and four-way frame clamp (D).

Paint Scraper

Used especially when stripping varnish.

Sanding Blocks

Wood, cork, or foam blocks that are used with sandpaper. They are used to apply an even pressure when sanding.

Tools for Clamping

Clamp

Steel instrument with two jaws, one movable and adjustable and the other fixed. Used to hold pieces in place.

Band Clamps

Used for clamping round pieces.

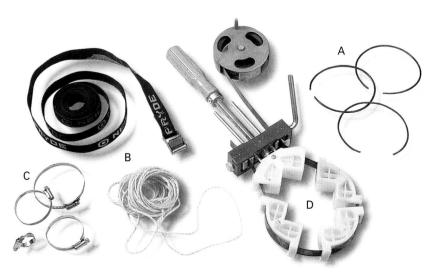

Power Tools and Bench Tools

Power Tools

Circular Saw

Used for ripping and crosscuts on all types of wood. It has a round blade with teeth for cutting. The base of the saw is placed on the piece and pushed forward as it cuts the wood.

Jigsaw

Used for cutting curves. The blades can be changed according to the material to be cut.

Electric Planer

Appropriate for large areas. Less precise than hand planes. It can make a deeper cut, reducing the time needed for the job

Electric Sander

Used for smoothing large areas or surfaces in very bad condition. Can be used with different grades of sandpaper. It is advisable to do the final sanding by hand, since the machine leaves small scratches on the wood.

Hot Glue Gun

Used for quick gluing when the joint does not have to support much weight.

Drill

Used for making holes. Drills quickly, and because it allows bits to be changed, it can make a variety of hole sizes.

Hot Air Gun

An appliance that blows hot air. Some have adjustable air and temperature. Used for stripping paint, they are very useful on vertical surfaces.

Electric Iron

This can be useful when veneering wood.

▲ Circular saw.

▲ Jigsaw.

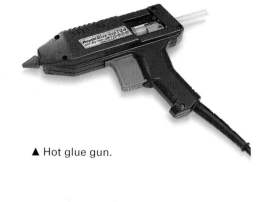

▲ Hot glue gun.

▲ Electric drill.

▲ Hot air gun.

▼ Electric sander.

▼ Electric iron.

▲ Electric hand planer.

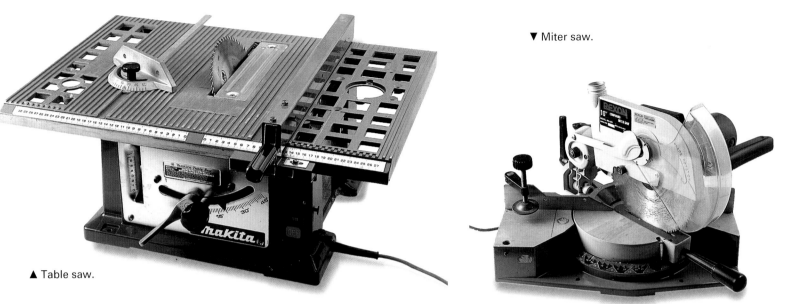

▲ Table saw.

▼ Miter saw.

Bench Tools

Table Saw and Miter Saw

These machines have a large work surface and cut quickly, which means that they require more attention and training for correct and safe use.

Bench Grinder

Used to sharpen hand tools, like chisels, gouges, and planes. It must be attached to the workbench.

Bench Vise

It is good to have a vise that is not attached to the bench, so it can be moved to hold an object in the most convenient position for working.

Workbench

This is the support for much of the work that is done during the restoration process, along with tables. Its top is from 6 to 8 feet (2 to 2.5 m) long, about 2 inches (10 cm) thick, and 32 to 36 inches (80 to 90 cm) high, supported by four legs braced with crosspieces. It has a vice for holding planks and pieces called dogs, which hold objects and keep them from moving around the bench top, as well as drawers and slots for storing tools, nails, measuring instruments, and so on.

▼ Bench grinder.

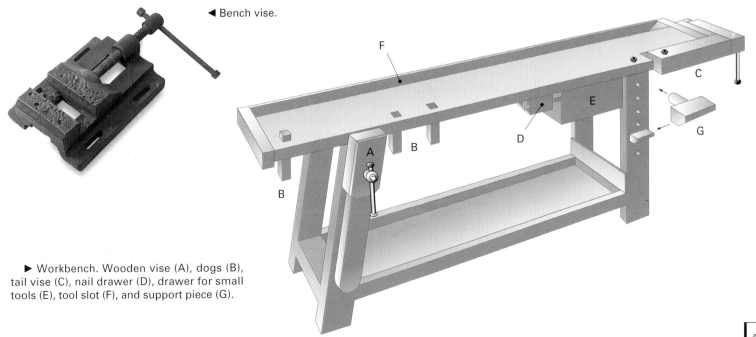

◄ Bench vise.

► Workbench. Wooden vise (A), dogs (B), tail vise (C), nail drawer (D), drawer for small tools (E), tool slot (F), and support piece (G).

Organization of the Work Space

DANGER SYMBOLS AND THEIR MEANINGS

Explosive Substances	E	**Danger:**	This sign indicates substances that can explode under certain conditions.
		Precaution:	Avoid shock, impact, friction, sparks, and heat.
Combustible Substances	O	**Danger:**	Oxidizing compounds can ignite combustible substances or can help spread existing fires, making them more difficult to extinguish.
		Precaution:	Avoid any contact with combustible substances.
Extremely Inflammable Substances	F+	**Danger:**	1. Liquids with a combustion point less than 32°F (0°C) and a boiling point less than 95°F (35°C).
		Precaution:	Avoid any contact with sources of ignition.
		Danger:	2. Gases, gas mixtures, and liquid gases that are very easily ignited at normal air pressure.
		Precaution:	Avoid the formation of inflammable gas-air mixtures and avoid sources of ignition.
Easily Inflammable Substances	F	**Danger:**	1. Self-igniting substances. Substances that ignite in contact with air.
		Precaution:	Avoid contact with air.
		Danger:	2. Substances sensitive to humidity. Chemicals that create fumes that are inflammable in contact with water.
		Precaution:	Avoid contact with humidity and water.
		Danger:	3. Liquids with an ignition point below 70°F (21°C).
		Precaution:	Isolate flames, heat sources, and sparks.
		Danger:	4. Solid substances that are easily ignited after short exposure to a source of ignition.
		Precaution:	Avoid all contact with sources of ignition.
Toxic and Very Toxic Substances	T T+	**Danger:**	These substances are very harmful if inhaled, swallowed, or come in contact with the skin, and they can even cause death. Therefore, this symbol indicates the possibility of irreversible damage from a single, repeated or short time exposure.
		Precaution:	Avoid bodily contact with the substance as well as the inhalation of fumes. In case of illness, contact a doctor.
Harmful Substances	Xn	**Danger:**	These substances are harmful if inhaled, swallowed, or come in contact with the skin. This symbol indicates the possibility of irreversible damage from a single, repeated, or short-time exposure.
		Precaution:	Avoid bodily contact with the substance as well as the inhalation of fumes. In case of illness, contact a doctor.
Corrosive Substances	C	**Danger:**	Living tissue and other materials are destroyed by contact with these substances.
		Precaution:	Do not inhale the fumes, and avoid contact with skin, eyes, and clothing.
Irritant Substances	Xi	**Danger:**	This symbol indicates those substances that can irritate the skin, the eyes, and the respiratory system.
		Precaution:	Do not inhale the fumes, and avoid contact with skin and eyes.
Substances That Are Harmful to the Environment	N	**Danger:**	Substances that over time can cause negative effects in the flora and fauna of any environment (aquatic and/or on land).
		Precaution:	Do not dispose of in the environment.

The correct organization of the work space is as important as the materials and tools used in the restoration process. A workshop laid out according to a few simple guidelines and kept in order creates pleasant working surroundings, and it will influence the quality and efficiency of the work.

It is preferable, if possible, to start with a large space, well ventilated and with natural light. Fluorescent tubes should be used for the general lighting of the space, and left turned on during all work hours. It is important to place a bright lightbulb over workbenches and tables to illuminate the work spaces. There should be electric outlets at each end of the workbench, next to the tables, and as close as possible to the machinery. In winter, the heat should be set on low, in order to avoid drying out certain products and to provide a comfortable temperature for physical work. The entrance door should be large and located on the ground floor, as close to the street as possible, to allow easier entry of furniture, machinery, and raw materials no matter how large and heavy they may be.

Toxic and Dangerous Materials

Inflammable and/or toxic products should be stored in a metal cabinet that can be locked; it should be located as far as possible from any heat sources. Containers should be completely closed to avoid evaporation, and they should be placed so that the warning labels are visible on opening the cabinet.

Woods and Veneers

Veneers should be stored in a cool, dry environment to keep them from becoming brittle. It is a good idea to place them on a flat board wrapped in newspaper to prevent their darkening from exposure to light, and under a second board to keep them flat. If slightly aged veneers are needed, it is not necessary to wrap them in newspapers. Wood pieces should be organized according to length and should be stored vertically, so that they will stay drier and will be easier to locate. Pieces that are in bad shape, full of nails, or have active wood beetles should be discarded.

▶ Tools commonly used in the shop are hung on a hook attached to the wall, where they are visible and easily accessible. A drawing of the tools' outlines can be a big help in staying organized.

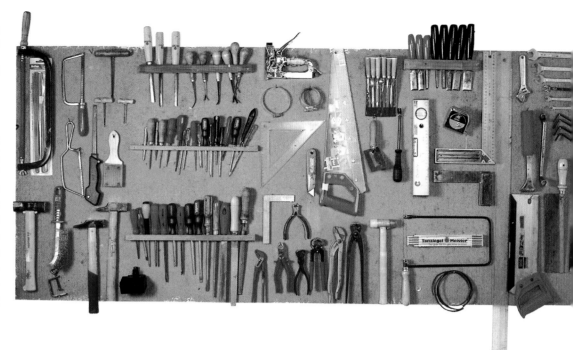

Benches and Tables

The wooden vise is normally located at one end of the workbench, so it is a good idea to place the bench far from walls or cabinets that could hinder work on large pieces. Tables should be strong and easy to clean. The tabletop should preferably be made of wood, to avoid scratching or denting objects that are being restored. Tables should be arranged so that they can be approached from all four sides, avoiding unnecessary movement of the pieces being restored.

Tools

The most frequently used tools should be located in a visible and easily accessible place. One practical solution is to hang them in an organized way on a board attached to the wall. Less frequently used tools can be kept in boxes or in furniture with drawers, made of wood if possible, to avoid damaging the blades of cutting tools. Power tools should be stored in plain sight on shelves, away from hand tools, to avoid accidents (like cutting electrical cords).

Machinery

Woodworking machines should be far away from the area where finishing is done, because they produce a great deal of dust and sawdust. They should always be well lit, and laid out in such a way that there is enough free space around them for their correct use.

Order, Storage, and Preservation

Supplies should be grouped by type, be in plain sight, and be correctly labeled or marked to avoid confusion. It is important to follow the manufacturer's directions for storage and preservation. After use, tools should be cleaned and put away, and they should always be kept sharpened.

Safety, Light, and Ventilation

To work safely at a project, it is necessary to have enough space for comfortable movement and good lighting. The ventilation should be constant, without causing cold or strong air currents. It is not advisable to store large amounts of scraps; therefore, small garbage bags are preferable to industrial size bags. Wastebaskets should always be kept closed. It is very important to have enough fire extinguishers for the size of the work space. They should be located in a visible and easily accessible place, and be maintained and inspected on a regular basis.

◀ Wood planks are stored on end and in order by height. This makes it easy to find and use them.

Technical *Aspects*

T he techniques used in restoring wood are just as varied as the objects being restored. They are often borrowed from such diverse fields as carpentry, painting, gilding, and metal working. Explanations of these techniques have been arranged in the order that they are carried out in the restoration process. This does not mean that a particular restoration project requires using all steps, but they will always be undertaken in this order. We begin by making a general evaluation of the problems we will face during the project, which will enable us to establish the required treatments and objectives. The first step in any intervention is the disassembly, protection, and storage of the parts. Different stripping techniques and specific treatments are the two steps to follow to prepare and repair the wood, leaving it ready for the final processes. The various carpentry tasks follow: techniques and systems of gluing, structural repair and replacement, addition of parts, veneer and marquetry. Final finishing, like filling, sanding, and waxing or lacquering, make up the next to last steps, and we finish with the assembly of parts, retouching small defects, and final cleaning.

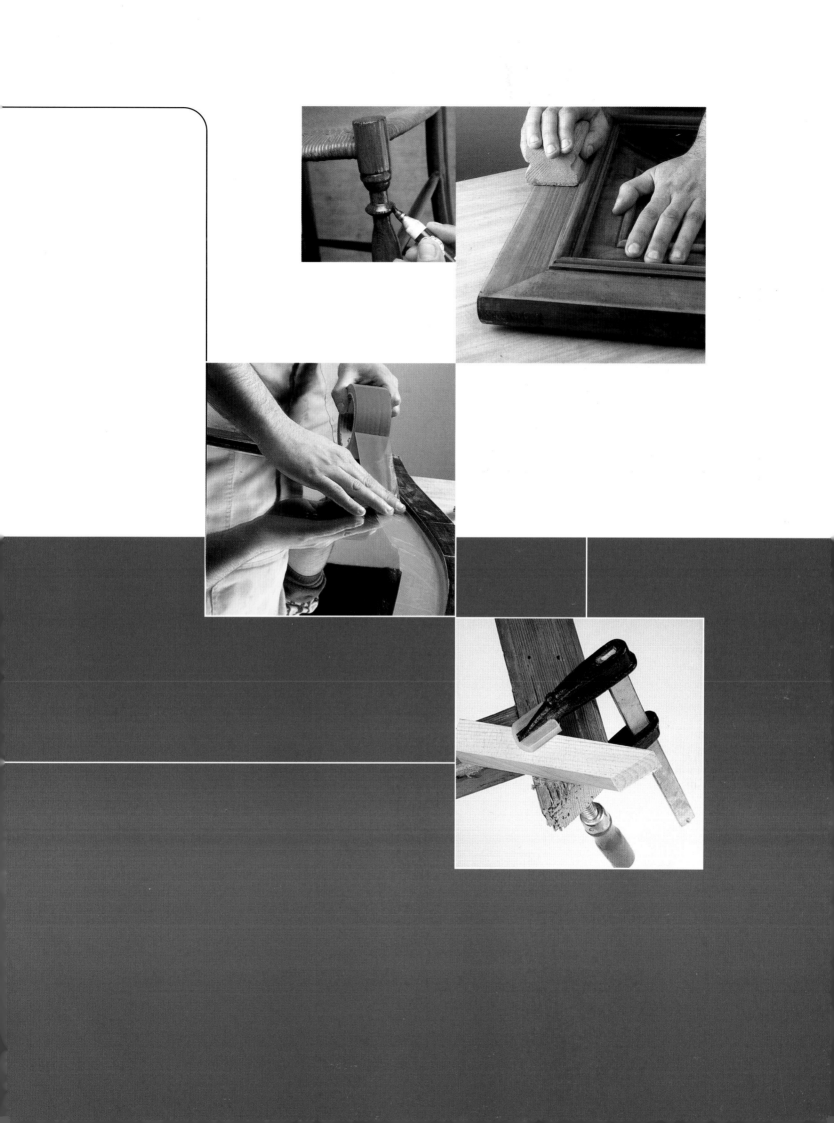

Evaluation

Before beginning the restoration of any piece of furniture or wooden structural element, we must make a complete and detailed diagnosis of possible problems, damage, or insect infestation affecting the piece. We should carefully note its general state of repair, based on a quick overall examination, then move on to list in order its characteristics and the condition of its various parts. The object should be examined from all angles (whenever possible), turning it, placing the base or bottom in a position to allow a thorough examination, removing parts like drawers and shelves. This study will be the tool that will allow an accurate restoration of the furniture or structural piece, seeing it as an object in which no part can stand out from the other, the quality of one finish over another, the function over the aesthetic value, or the aesthetics over its possible use.

The Steps of the Diagnostic Evaluation Process

Study of the Carpentry Tasks

The carpentry tasks will always depend on the type of furniture or element that is being restored, and repair will be governed by the object as well as by one's own experience. Let's look at some examples.

With chairs, it is especially important to evaluate the frames and joints, the strength of the glued parts, and the condition of the legs.

Dressers usually have problems with the structure (where the frame has pulled apart), the tops (boards separated as a result of brusque changes in relative humidity), and the drawers (poor fit).

With wardrobes, the condition of the frame especially should be evaluated, the condition and fit of the doors, and the condition of the hinges.

In any case, we will also take note of missing parts and moldings, lost veneer, inlay, and marquetry, and minor cracking and breakage.

Insect Infestation

The piece being restored should be examined for signs of infestation (especially beetle and termite). If there are any signs, it is very important to find out if there is present activity or just the traces of past attacks. In the former case, the appropriate treatment should be undertaken.

General Condition of the Wood

Note the overall condition of the wood the object is made of.

Period

The period during which the object was made gives us valuable information about its construction and the kinds of finishes that we can elect to use.

Type

Based on the type of object, rustic or sophisticated, we can decide on certain details of restoration.

Hardware

It is important to determine whether there are missing locks, keyholes, rings, pulls or knobs, and keys. There can also be chipped and broken marble and missing or broken small decorative parts and mirrors.

▼ **Evaluation of an Alphonsine-style dining table.**

1. This type of square table can be extended by sliding the top apart on supports under the table top and placing one or more leaves in the middle. Our inspection has proven the strength of the table (legs, braces, cross-pieces, and joints) and that the mechanism works properly. The loss of some small parts and small areas of veneer is observed, especially on the table top.

▲ **2.** A lateral crosspiece is the part of the table that shows the greatest amount of damage. After a general evaluation, we have decided that it is neither necessary nor desirable to replace it, since it is strong enough for daily use of the table. The aesthetic value and uniformity of all the wood in the table are also important. In this case, we will proceed with a curative repair of the piece.

▶ **Evaluating a rustic table.**

In contrast to the case of the mirror (below), the evaluation of a rustic pine table suggests that some of its parts should be replaced. The central crosspiece and the lateral crosspiece to which it is joined have splintered and lost a great amount of material through insect infestation. Because of this they have completely lost their strength and their bracing function. Since these are simple elements that are part of a rustic furniture piece made of plain wood, we will consider replacing them completely.

◀ **Inspecting hidden areas.**

It is important to closely examine all parts of the object. In this case, we evaluate an antique dresser, inspecting the frame from the inside, the back side, and the bottom by turning it upside down.

Conclusions

After the evaluation process we move on to the restoration of the object. Restored furniture and objects should be used and fulfill the function for which they were designed. All original parts should be preserved, where possible, and should only be replaced when use or function is affected. Similarly, only missing parts of inlay and marquetry should be replaced. Accessory pieces like marble, pulls, keyholes and mirrors should be kept and simply cleaned. Whenever possible, repairs should be reversible. The restoration work should not affect the quality of the piece, and the materials and workmanship must never be inferior to the quality of the original.

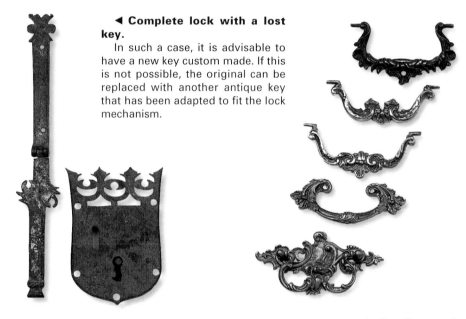

◀ **Complete lock with a lost key.**

In such a case, it is advisable to have a new key custom made. If this is not possible, the original can be replaced with another antique key that has been adapted to fit the lock mechanism.

▲ **Handles and pulls.**

It is very important to keep these parts, especially if they are originals. Sometimes hardware will add value to a piece of common furniture.

▶ **Mirror belonging to an Alphonsine-style washstand.**

This has been kept just as it was before restoration, following the guidelines that discourage replacement of antique mirrors. If the old mirror had been replaced, the restoration would have diminished the value of the piece as a work of art, thereby affecting the final quality.

▲ Types of keys

In order to match a key of the same period and style to the lock, it is a good idea to keep a small collection of different kinds of keys in the shop.

◄ ▲ Keyholes

Like knobs and pulls, keyholes have a tendency to get lost, so furniture often comes to the shop without them. Having a small collection can remedy this problem.

Choice of Treatment

Once the preliminary evaluation of the piece to be restored is done, we will select the proper treatment based on our information and conclusions. This will give us a general idea of the series and order of the processes required to restore the specific object. Complete removal of hardware and accessories, stripping, filling or reinforcing material, repair or replacement and gluing of parts, color matching, and covering defects, surface preparation, and final finishing are the required steps in all restoration projects.

▼ It is a good idea to keep the original lock, repairing it whenever necessary. In the event that it has to be changed, it should be replaced with another of the same period.

▼ Marquetry done with two kinds of veneer, of different colors. Only veneer is used in marquetry, so that the different woods are all at the same height.

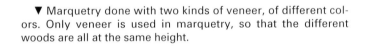

◄ Marquetry work done with different stained wood veneers. In the event that some pieces become lost, only the missing areas should be replaced.

▲ Mother of pearl keyhole inlaid into the solid box. If there is partial damage to the piece, the missing area should be reconstructed using the same material.

▲ Inlay work of wood strips and pieces of mother of pearl in a wood box. The inlay is done by inserting small pieces of diverse materials (mother of pearl, bone, ivory…) and/or wood strips in solid wood. If it is to be restored, the missing pieces should be replaced with small pieces of the same material and color as the originals.

▲ Inlaid marquetry of a strip made of zinc and wood.

► Inlay strips missing from an object being restored can be replaced by similar ones that are sold ready-made. If similar pieces cannot be found, they should be produced in the shop.

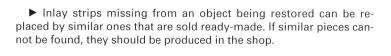

Before Restoration Begins

Before the actual restoration process, which begins with stripping, it is very important to remove, protect, and store certain pieces.

To work efficiently, one must remove all of the parts that could impede such operations as stripping, sanding, scraping, polishing… These components collect dirt where they are attached to the wood, and they can adversely affect the quality of the work. Other parts usually require different treatment from that of the wood object; therefore, they must be removed so they can be treated appropriately.

Removable Parts

Removable parts can be connectors (hinges…), locking devices (locks, keyholes…), decorative (pulls, small parts, marble pieces…), and structural (drawers, shelves…). They should all be individually marked, making a similar mark on the part of the wood where it is to be replaced. If they are small, they should be kept in bags or boxes clearly marked with the name of the object they belong to, what part of the object, and the number of pieces. Marble and table tops should be marked on the underside, and always in order. Drawers should be marked on the outside rear, always in order, and marked with the same symbol in the corresponding place, on the inside of the furniture piece.

▲ It is very important to mark all parts as they are removed. Markings should be made on the wood and on the part; in some cases, one can indicate the part's orientation. In this case, upon removing the hinge from a door we see that there is already a mark there that surely served as a guide for the manufacturer, and it will be preserved.

▼ All removed parts should be marked and stored conveniently classified in bags. In them there should be a paper noting the furniture piece or object they came from.

▼ Protective tape for glass, metal, and fabrics. It leaves no residue or mark on the protected surface when removed.

Parts That Cannot Be Removed

There are parts that should not be removed, because they are fragile or because it would be too complicated. Therefore it is a good idea to very carefully protect them from possible bumping and damage from chemicals. These items could be: glass, mirrors, certain marbles, some types of keyholes, upholstery….

Because of their fragility, glass and mirrors are the elements that require the greatest protection. Once they are perfectly clean, protective tape is placed on the inside of the perimeter, ensuring complete adherence. This way, possible scratching during sanding is avoided. When aggressive chemicals are not to be used, the surface of the glass or mirror should be protected with newspaper fixed with masking tape. If such products (solvents, oxalic acid…) are to be used, glass should be protected with plastic bubble wrap taped over the tape that was placed around the perimeter.

Metal parts should be covered with protective tape for glass or masking tape. Marble and upholstery should also be protected with plastic bubble wrap or fixed with masking tape.

▲ Protecting mirrors.
1. Thorough cleaning of glass and mirrors is the first step in their protection.

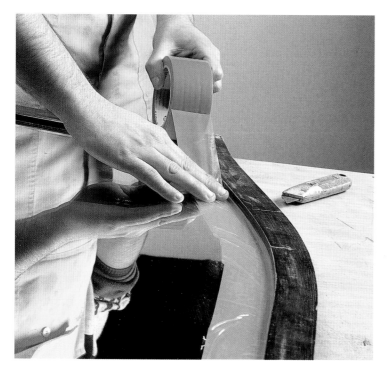

▲ 3. It is important to protect all the angles and joints of the mirror to avoid possible leakage of chemicals.

▲ 2. The outside edge of the mirror is carefully covered with protective tape, paying special attention to the curved areas.

▶ 4. Plastic bubble wrap is affixed to the special protective tape with masking tape. This assures total protection from bumping and chemicals.

▼ Protecting fabric

1. All pieces of upholstery and fabrics should be very carefully protected because they could acquire stains that can be impossible to eliminate. In this case, the cover of a game table is being protected. First, the inside edges are covered with protective tape.

▶ 2. In this case, protective plastic is required because the chemicals that will be used could stain the original cover.

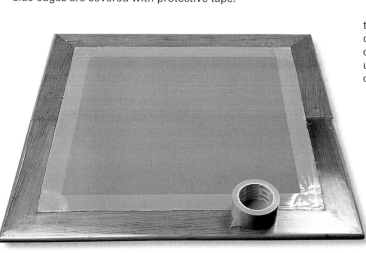

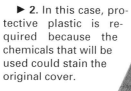

Stripping

In a great many cases, it will be necessary to strip the wood that is to be restored. A piece may have a thick coat of paint hiding the original high quality wood; another may have large areas of a mismatched color. A piece of furniture that was originally finished with a dark varnish might now be more attractive with a natural wood finish. These are some of the cases when stripping is needed.

Stripping techniques can be divided into two groups according to the method employed: mechanical and chemical. Mechanical methods are based on the use of different tools and materials that remove a layer of paint or varnish by mechanical means: electric sanding, hand scraping, hand sanding, using scrapers and awls, and the hot air gun. Chemical stripping methods remove the coating using different products that cause a chemical reaction to soften the finish, which is then removed. They are alcohol, caustic soda, and solvents.

The stripping techniques used will depend on the kind of wood, its condition, the kind of varnish or paint to be removed, and the desired result. Work should always begin with the least aggressive method and then proceed to more efficient methods.

▼ Hand sanding carved parts.
1. Hand sanding a decorative carved flower. Using a simple sheet of sandpaper, we remove the dark varnish from between the petals.

◄ Electric sanding.
Electric sanding is highly recommended for stripping large areas, and always recommended for flat surfaces. In this case, it is used on the flat backrest of a chair, whose square bars are completely flat. This sanding goes quickly.

Mechanical Stripping

Electric Sanding
This is most appropriate for stripping flat areas and large surfaces. Different grits of paper can be used with electric sanders to achieve a perfectly clean surface.

Blade Scraping
This is a slower method than hand sanding, using different types of scraper blades (straight or shaped). It is used for solid wood whose condition is not very good, for shaped solid wood (rungs, legs...), and for smoothing.

Hand Sanding
The sandpaper is used directly on the wood, rubbing vigorously. It should be used on wood that has a light coat of paint or varnish.

◄ Hand scraping.
Scraping the rounded bars of the backrest of a solid wood chair.

▼ 2. Hand sanding the deep groove of a molding by wrapping sandpaper around a finger.

▲ **3.** Sometimes it is necessary to use auxiliary items to achieve a good sanding. A piece of dowel (always found in a shop) helps in hand sanding grooves.

▲ **4.** A piece of folded sandpaper will be needed to finish hand sanding angled surfaces.

▲ **5.** The use of folded sandpaper is the only way to hand sand very fine and elaborate molding.

Scrapers and Gravers

Scrapers and gravers work well in very complicated areas. They are used in curved places or moldings and in small, difficult to reach grooves. They also can be used when the layer to be removed is very hard and requires some force.

Hot Air Gun

A hot air gun is used to strip solid wood with heavy coats of paint. It is especially appropriate for structural elements like doors and beams, because it can clean large areas in a short amount of time. It is important to use a gun with separate air flow and temperature regulators, so as not to burn and blacken the wood. The hot air on the wood makes the paint soften and blister, allowing it to be easily removed with a paint scraper.

▲ **Stripping with gravers.**
1. Gravers are used to scrape darkened varnish from curved and scrolled depressions and molding.

▲ **2.** Varnish in the small decorative cuts of the petals can also be removed with a graver.

▶ **Stripping with a hot air gun.**
Removing a thick coat of paint from solid wood with a hot air gun. This system does an efficient job in a short time.

▲ **Cleaning with a scraper.**
Scraping a flat surface that has a very hard layer of varnish. The scraper achieves a good finish on the right angles of the molding on this drawer.

Chemical Stripping

Alcohol

Using alcohol as a chemical stripper is highly recommended because of its advantages: It is not toxic to the user, and it is inexpensive. Alcohol does not damage wood and it evaporates quickly, so it can be used on veneers and marquetry because it will not loosen the veneer. It is generously applied with a pad of lint free cotton strands or cheesecloth; after the varnish has softened, proceed by removing it with a clean, new pad.

Caustic Soda

A caustic soda solution is used on solid pine (the only wood that can take such an aggressive procedure) and never on veneered areas or marquetry. The water in the solution would soften the glue and loosen the veneer and pieces of marquetry.

The solution should be mixed in a bucket diluting 2 pounds (1 kg) of caustic soda for each gallon (5 liters) of hot water, stirring until it is totally dissolved. The solution is applied to the wood with a saturated cotton pad. Squeeze it out over the surface to be treated until it is evenly spread and thoroughly soaked. It is removed by rinsing the wood with tap water using clean cotton strands or rags, always following the grain of the wood.

Caustic soda is an irritant (as is indicated by the international symbol on the label). It is necessary to use long neoprene gloves, a respirator for fumes, safety glasses, and heavy clothing. Apply it in a well-ventilated place.

Commercial Solvents

Commercial solvents are widely used, and on many kinds of wood. The product is applied with a brush, then left to work for a length of time determined by the type of varnish or paint that needs to be removed. The paint is scraped and removed with a paint scraper, and cotton strands or rags impregnated with alcohol or turpentine are used to remove any traces of the chemical. All chemical solvents are irritants and toxic; therefore, the use of neoprene gloves and a respirator is required.

▲ Stripping walnut burl veneers on drawer fronts with alcohol. The alcohol is applied and removed using clean cotton strands or rags.

◄ Stripping a solid pine structural element with caustic soda. The mixture is removed by rinsing with tap water until all traces of the paint are gone.

◄ Using a commercial stripper on the front of a drawer that has a thin layer of old paint.

On certain occasions the wood itself requires special treatments apart from carpentry work. These treatments affect some of the characteristics of the wood, like its hardness, its surface, or its color.

Filling the Wood

When the wood has lost a great deal of its natural rigidity and hardness it is necessary to fill it in. Normally it suffers this great loss from damage caused by wood-boring insects.

It can also be caused by wood rot due to excessive water or humidity, but not as often. It is a good idea to avoid replacing areas of damaged wood, so wood filling treatments are recommended to repair small areas of missing material.

The filling process consists of applying a wax that hardens at room temperature, or applying two-part synthetic resins. The wax is a mixture of pure beeswax with paraffin and a dye similar to the color of the wood to be filled. The mixture is heated in a double boiler until it is completely liquefied, and immediately poured onto the area of the wood to be treated, since it hardens at room temperature. Once it hardens, it can be sanded, and it is completely reversible by applying heat.

The application of two-part resins takes place once the parts are mixed according to the ratios stated on the manufacturer's label. These resins also harden quickly at room temperature but can be worked when they are still soft. They can later be worked and stained, but their major drawback is that they are completely irreversible.

▲ **Filling with wax.**
1. Minor loss of material on a pine surface. There are only small holes on the side of a piece of furniture; therefore, we decide to fill it with wax.

▲ **2.** We have made a mixture of pure beeswax, paraffin, and stain, which is heated in a double boiler until it melts completely. The liquid is then applied directly on each hole with a spoon.

▶ **3.** The lumps of wax are spread and smoothed using a spatula. The wax will quickly solidify at room temperature, allowing a final sanding to even out the high areas on the surface.

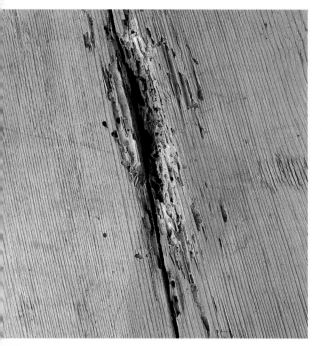

◄ **Filling with resins.**

1. There is a significant loss of material due to wood-boring insects at the seam between two boards in a piece of furniture.

◄ **2.** The sides are taped (in this case, it is necessary to tape only one side) at the area where the resin will be applied, to control splashing and dripping. Once the two-part resin is mixed, in the indicated ratio, it is applied with the help of a small wooden stick.

◄ **3.** The resin hardens quickly at room temperature and it is a good idea to begin scraping it while it is still setting.

► **4.** Once hardened, a cut is made to match the filled part with the rest of the surface, which has an obvious separation between the boards. Later the resin will be stained to match the color of the wood.

► **Rebuilding with resins.**
Besides filling wood and covering small holes, two-part resins are used to rebuild large pieces of wood. In this case, this material is used to fill a structural piece that is very damaged by insect action and to replace material in one area to be able to level the unevenness of the wood.

Bleaching Wood

Sometimes it will be necessary to bleach the wood, to restore the piece to its original state or achieve an attractive finish. Some of the situations requiring a bleaching of this kind include: a furniture piece made of various woods with different tones, streaks, and traces of paint or stains that have penetrated the pores of the wood.

Normally, we use hydrogen peroxide (oxygenated water: H_2O_2) at 30% solution by weight or volume, or a supersaturated oxalic acid solution dissolved in water. The hydrogen peroxide bleaches by oxidizing and "burning" the surface of the wood, resulting in a whitish tone.

► Hydrogen peroxide (oxygenated water) and oxalic acid are used for bleaching wood. The latter is very useful in removing ink stains from drawers, boards, and desk tops.

Oxalic acid is the most widely used product for bleaching. It is always used in a supersaturated water solution (it will separate and settle in the bottom of the container). It is used on surfaces that are not damaged by the liberal use of water. It is applied with a brush, and left to dry completely on the wood. The water in the solution evaporates during drying, causing the oxalic acid to crystallize on the surface. To remove it, the surface is rinsed with plenty of plain water. This raises the grain of the wood, so it is necessary to finish the process with a thorough sanding.

▼ **Bleaching with oxalic acid.**
1. Wood that is varnished or painted and stained in dark tones usually has great color differences and very darkened pores. A simple stripping often will not return the wood to its natural color. This drawer, already stripped, still presents major color differences.

▼ **2.** A supersaturated solution of oxalic acid in water is applied with a brush (since it is a large surface) and allowed to dry completely.

▼ **3.** The traces of oxalic acid that appear on the surface of the wood are thoroughly cleaned. It is wiped with a lot of water with the help of a cotton rag. Once it is dry, the surface is sanded, because the cleaning with water has raised the grain of the wood.

▼ The large top of a rustic table is stained with a water-based stain to achieve a deep, dark color in accordance with the style of the furniture piece. The stain is applied with a sponge, which helps achieve a uniform tone and saves time and effort.

Staining Wood

Sometimes we want a color different than that of the original wood. For this we will resort to stains. There are two kinds of stains used in wood restoration: water based and alcohol based.

Water-based stains are made by dissolving aniline dye in hot water and then letting it cool. If this stain is prepared in large quantities, it is a good idea to add a little bleach to prevent bacterial growth. Since it is mixed with a solvent (the water), which evaporates very evenly, it allows very even applications and deepening of tone or color by successive layering. The water raises the grain of the wood and, therefore, requires a

final polishing. This should be done with a brush with soft vegetable bristles, because rubbing with sandpaper would remove some of the color.

Alcohol-based stains are a solution of aniline dye and alcohol. This type of solvent evaporates very quickly and requires great skill to achieve uniform areas of color without streaking.

A brush is used to apply stain in small or nonhorizontal areas. On broad flat surfaces, the use of a sponge is recommended. Aniline stains are sold as powders in different colors, so an infinite number of mixed colors can be made.

Carpentry

Woodworking surely requires the use of the most diverse techniques in the restoration process. Restoration carpentry covers various processes: joining, repairing, adding material, and applying adhesives.

Glues and Gluing Techniques

The first step in gluing, in any restoration project, is the total removal of any bits of old glues and all traces of dirt, which will guarantee an efficient adhesion of the parts. Keep in mind that it is very important to check the fit of all parts, testing them before applying the glue.

There are many types of glue, which are appropriate for different uses. The most useful for different projects is white glue or PVA (polyvinyl acetate). It comes ready to use, is water soluble, and is easy to apply. Its drawbacks are the drying time (24 hours) and the fact that it is visible. It is the best product for gluing joints.

Traditional carpenter's glue (made from animal parts) is transparent and dissolves the old glue (it is applied hot), so it is not necessary to remove the old glue. It is used less and less because of its complex preparation and difficulty of application.

Glues based on cyanoacrylates are fine for gluing small parts and decorations. But they cannot be placed under tension or support any kind of weight.

Hot glue is applied with a gun, and can be used as a filler material (a loose dowel, for example) and to quickly glue small parts. Its greatest disadvantage is that it adheres instantly, which can create problems.

Two-part glues are appropriate for joining two pieces that are missing material. They are sold ready to use, and it is important to follow the manufacturer's instructions. Once dry, they can be cut, sanded, and stained.

Although it seems quite handy, the use of contact cement is not advised, because it does not allow any margin for moving and adjusting the parts.

The most widely used joinery technique is the gluing of pieces using clamps. These permit a strong bond between parts that are straight and always on the same plane. One variation is the four-way frame clamp, often used for frames and objects whose joints are at right angles, as in the case of a chair or the frame of a piece of furniture. A tourniquet is used for gluing together parts that are curved or angled (common in chairs). Heavy twine or a rope is used, because it has to apply the force necessary to make a strong joint. The pressure on the joints is controlled by inserting a piece of wood between two strands of rope and twisting as needed.

▼ Glue is usually applied with a brush. Putting white glue on both parts assures a strong joint for a completely disjointed chair rung.

▼ Applying glue with the help of a syringe is very useful when there are areas that are difficult to get to with a brush. In this case, the glue is injected in the small free space between the mortise and the tenon of the chair; this permits us to glue a loose joint.

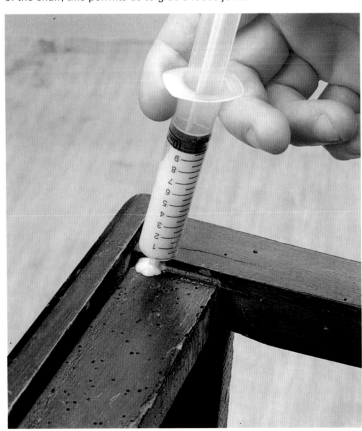

◄ It is a good idea to use a paint roller to apply glue to large surfaces. This technique is used on large sheets of veneer in marquetry work.

▼ Four-way frame clamps are used for joining right angles. In this case, a chair with a rectangular frame and square legs is being glued.

► Clamps allow new pieces to be joined to the existing wood, as well as efficient gluing of assemblies on the same plane. It is a good idea to place protective pieces between the clamps and the object.

► The tourniquet method is useful for holding joints that are curved or not parallel. This method is most often used on chairs, because of their complex structure. The tourniquet is a quick and easy way to hold complicated joints, exerting force as the cord is twisted around a stick. In this case, the tourniquet is holding the leg joints to the backrest.

Structural Repair

Every restoration project requires structural and mechanical repairs that are as unique and different as the objects being repaired. Even though we are faced with diverse challenges, there are some cases, like the repair of legs and drawers, that are commonly seen.

◄ Repairing a leg

1. The leg has suffered a heavy insect attack and has lost a great amount of material. In fact, this part of the table cannot fulfill its supporting function; therefore, it has to be replaced.

► 2. A diagonal cut is made just above the damaged part, using a piece of wood as a guide to support the saw.

◄ 4. The shape of the cut is marked on the new piece of wood with a pencil. A board clamped to the leg will act as a guide to assure correct alignment.

▲ 3. A piece of wood held with a clamp will act as a guide for making a second diagonal cut perpendicular to the first one. By making an angular cut in the wood, a larger surface is achieved than with a simple cross cut, thus enlarging the gluing surface with the new piece. The narrower the angle cut the stronger the joint will be.

► 5. Then the new piece is shaped, glue is spread on both pieces of the wood, and the joint is secured using a clamp. A proper gluing job requires 24 hours to dry.

▲ Repairing a drawer.
1. Because of their heavy use, drawers tend to break easily, so it is common to repair them in restoration projects. One of the guides of this drawer is worn out.

▶ 2. The first step in the restoration consists of using a miter saw to remove the remains of the guide and other pieces that extend over the board that forms the bottom of the drawer.

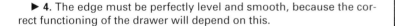

▲ 3. The edge is leveled and smoothed using a chisel and a plane.

▶ 4. The edge must be perfectly level and smooth, because the correct functioning of the drawer will depend on this.

▼ 5. Because the board covering the bottom of the drawer has also been damaged (it is thinner at the edge than in the middle), a piece of wood is glued to both edges to secure it. Then it should be planed smooth.

▼ 6. The final step in the process is gluing the drawer guide. It should be the same width as the one on the other side and at the front of the drawer.

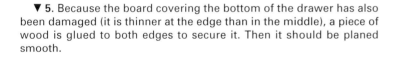

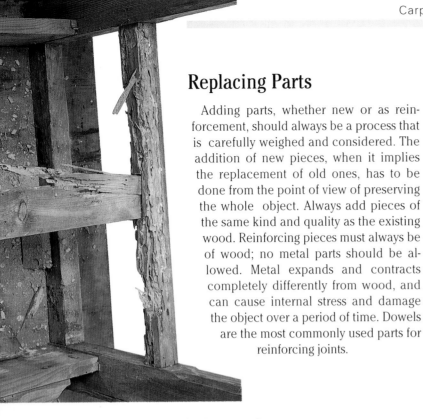

Replacing Parts

Adding parts, whether new or as reinforcement, should always be a process that is carefully weighed and considered. The addition of new pieces, when it implies the replacement of old ones, has to be done from the point of view of preserving the whole object. Always add pieces of the same kind and quality as the existing wood. Reinforcing pieces must always be of wood; no metal parts should be allowed. Metal expands and contracts completely differently from wood, and can cause internal stress and damage the object over a period of time. Dowels are the most commonly used parts for reinforcing joints.

▲ Replacing and reinforcing crosspieces.
1. The long crosspiece and the lateral crosspiece of a table have been greatly damaged by insects. The loss of material is so great that the table has broken. Replacing the pieces will allow it to become useful again.

▲ 2. The lateral crosspiece is cut by sawing flush with the leg. Next, the table's long crosspiece will be removed.

◄ 3. A new crosspiece is made. A piece of the same kind of wood as that to be replaced should be cut to the same dimensions. We measure the placement and dimensions of the joint using calipers. Once the new piece is marked, we begin to cut out the mortise with a chisel.

▼ 4. Finally, a piece is cut to the appropriate dimensions for an exact fit between the legs.

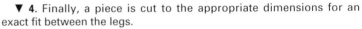

◄ **5.** The long crosspiece is made in the same way. A tenon is cut at either end with a chisel and saw, to fit into the lateral crosspiece.

▼ **6.** Before gluing the new pieces in place, it is necessary to check the fit of the mortise and tenon. It is also necessary to check the fit between the long crosspiece and the original lateral crosspiece.

▲ **7.** Next, white glue is applied with a brush.

► **8.** The new pieces are held in place with clamps. They are arranged to apply force in the same direction as the long crosspiece and the lateral crosspiece. One is placed at a perpendicular angle to hold the glued crosspiece at the correct angle.

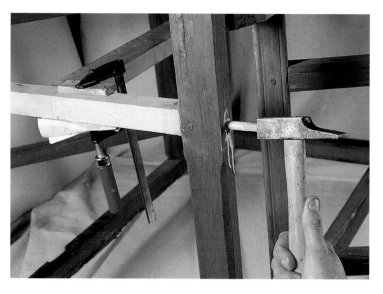

▲ **9.** Since the lateral crosspiece is only joined to the legs at the ends, it is a good idea to reinforce the joints. To this end, a hole is drilled through each leg into the crosspiece.

▲ **10.** A wooden dowel is hammered into place to act as a reinforcement. The glue helps hold the reinforcing piece to the two pieces of wood.

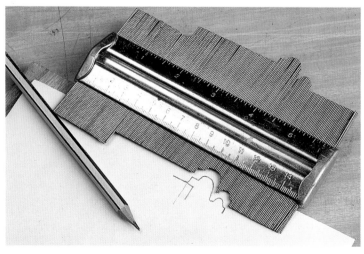

▲ **A template for molding.**

1. Lost pieces of molding are a common problem in restoring wood objects. In this case, an entire piece of molding is missing from a door.

▲ **2.** By placing a profile gauge perpendicular to the molding and pushing down on it, the profile can be copied.

◄ **3.** Making a template for cutting is simple: Just trace the profile on the paper.

▲ Drawer backs.
1. Other parts that are commonly replaced are the backs of drawers. In these cases, it is necessary to make a part with dovetails that will fit perfectly into the original side pieces of the drawer.

▲ 2. Dovetails are used in drawers because they stand up well to the pulling forces that can be placed on them. They are based on joining trapezoidal mortises and tenons that are impossible to slide apart.

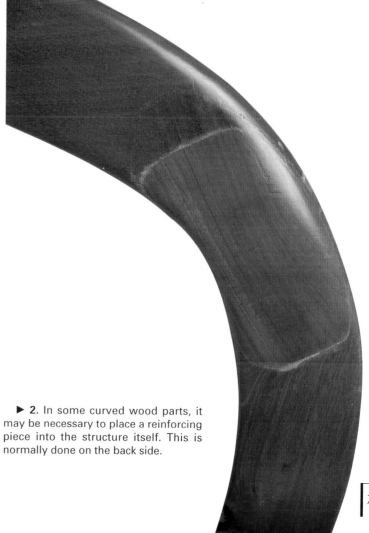

▲ Braces.
1. Placing an angle brace inside the leg and frame assembly of a chair is a common practice. In the same way, an angle piece can be used to reinforce the rungs and the legs.

▶ 2. In some curved wood parts, it may be necessary to place a reinforcing piece into the structure itself. This is normally done on the back side.

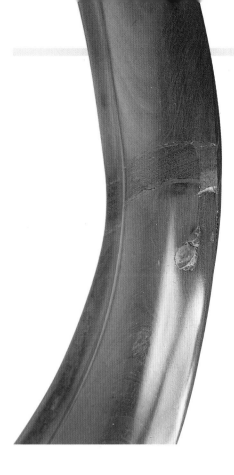

◄ **3.** It is also common to add reinforcement to a curved piece for transversal strength, as in the case of this dowel.

► **4.** It is usual to strengthen chair joints (where they carry all of the weight) by inserting a dowel.

Veneer and Marquetry

To repair an area that is missing veneer, the area of the break must be cleaned. Carefully make a straight cut with a veneer saw, then remove the remains of broken veneer and glue. Cut a piece of veneer the same size as the break, using a piece that is as close as possible to the original veneer. Apply white glue to the veneer, and ensure good adhesion by pressing with a hot iron; this will cause the evaporation of the water contained in the glue.

Replacing one or several pieces of inlay first requires a thorough cleaning of the existing groove or cut, or else making a new one in the wood. Once the damaged area is perfectly clean, we begin to select or make the pieces that are to be inlaid. These can be of different materials (wood, bone, metal) and in any number of shapes. Because of this, most of the time they will have to be custom-made in the shop. However, some ready-made shapes are available on the market, like boxwood strips.

Once the pieces are selected and made, we place them into the wood surface with white glue, and insert them with the help of a hammer or awl until they are level with the surface of the wood. The drying process can be accelerated by applying heat with an iron.

Replacing a missing piece of inlay is done by tracing its shape with the help of carbon paper. It is then transferred to the chosen sheet of veneer, which is then strengthened by gluing a piece of paper to the back with rabbit-skin glue. It is very important to keep in mind that the back where the paper reinforcement is glued will be, at the end of the process, the face of the veneer that will be visible when the repair is completed. Once the paper with the shape of the missing piece is affixed to the veneer, it is cut with the veneer saw, then glued to the surface to be restored. The process ends with the removal of the paper and glue with water and a final sanding of the piece.

▼ **Repairing veneer.**
1. Once the damaged area is smoothed and cleaned, choose and cut a piece of veneer that is as similar as possible to the missing piece.

▲ **2.** The missing piece is glued on, and a final sanding smoothes the surface.

▲ **Repairing inlay.**

Once the area needing repair is clean, the required length of boxwood strip is cut. White glue is applied and the inlay is then placed with the help of an awl or other tool according to the shape of the piece to be inlaid. The bond is activated by applying heat with an iron.

▲ **Repairing marquetry work.**

1. The first step is to remove the remaining traces of glue and veneer by scraping with an awl.

▲ **2.** To trace the shape of the replacement piece use carbon paper, a sheet of white paper, and a blunt object for applying pressure.

◀ **3.** Then, the carbon paper is placed clean side down over the marquetry and secured with tape. The sheet of paper is placed over the carbon paper and is also affixed with tape. Pressure is applied using the handle of a tool to achieve an outline.

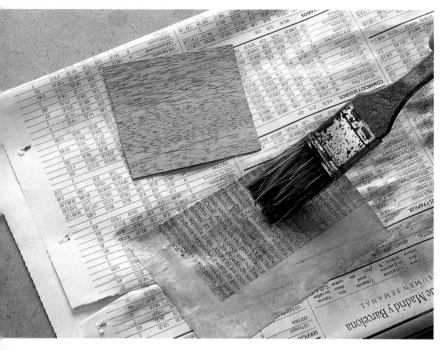

▲ 4. We choose a piece of veneer that is as close as possible to the existing marquetry in color, texture, and grain. To stiffen and strengthen it, we glue it to a piece of newsprint with rabbit-skin glue.

▲ 5. The tracing is glued to the other side of the veneer in the same manner. Then, we make it easier to work with by attaching a stack of veneer sheets with masking tape.

▼ 6. We clamp it to the workbench, and make a small hole with a hand drill, which will be used to insert the saw blade for an easy and clean cut.

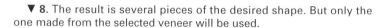

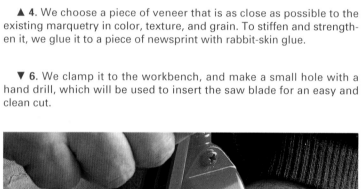

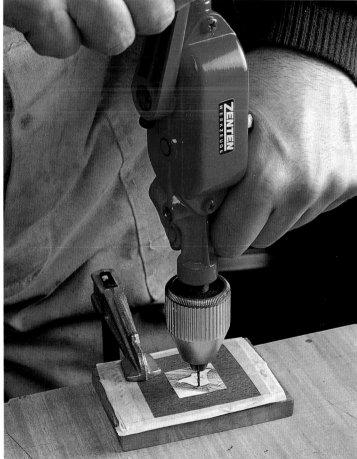

▲ 7. Using a fret saw, with a fine marquetry blade, we carefully cut out the shape.

▼ 8. The result is several pieces of the desired shape. But only the one made from the selected veneer will be used.

▲ 9. The piece will be replaced using rabbit-skin glue. The side with the newsprint glued to it will be facing up.

▶ 10. We protect the marquetry with paper and a thick wood board, and hold the glued piece in place with a clamp.

▼ 11. The paper is removed by rubbing it with a rag slightly dampened with water.

▼ 12. A final sanding will make the piece level with the rest.

Finishing the Object

The finish is just as important as the process of restoring the wood object. The choice of the finish will depend on the evaluation (period, style, type…) and the value (aesthetic, monetary…) that we wish to give to it. The finish can either enhance or detract from the restoration that has been done to this point; therefore, an in-depth analysis will be necessary to choose a finish, and then great attention must be paid to its execution.

Covering Minor Defects

Only small holes caused by the action of parasites, small losses of material, or minor superficial cracks should be covered. Otherwise, we will be dealing with specific carpentry or wood filling projects.

For repairing holes or small amounts of missing surface material, it is a good idea to use fillers. Two-part fillers are available premixed or for mixing in the workshop. They can be applied over the imperfection with a spatula, smoothing it and scraping off the excess. All fillers shrink and contract upon drying, so repair will require several applications and subsequent drying, building up to the level of the surrounding material. A final sanding will remove excess filler and will blend it into the surface of the wood. Because the filler is applied just before the finish (varnish, wax, or lacquer), it is important to select a tone similar to that which the wood will have after being finished. To establish the color of the wood, wet it with alcohol (it will not leave streaks or rings, evaporates quickly, and does not damage the wood); in this way you are sure to get the correct color and tone for the filler.

The best way to fill small holes resulting from insect attacks is to use hard wax. This is applied after the wood has received its final finish (wax or varnish), making the choice of color and tone quite easy. Hard waxes come in sticks in many shades, and they can be mixed. Pinch off a small quantity from the stick and knead it with your fingers; the warmth will soften the wax, forming a pointed cylinder. It is applied with the help of a wood spatula, if possible of the same or lesser hardness than the wood being repaired, to avoid scratching it.

▲ **Filler.**
1. For filling small losses of material (insect holes) and superficial wood cracks. A two-part filler is applied with the help of a spatula. Several applications are necessary; the filler contracts when it dries.

◀ **2.** Once the filler has dried, it is sanded to remove the excess filler and to level the surface with that of the wood.

◀ **Hard wax.**
The small holes left by insects often must be repaired with hard wax, because it can be applied after the wood has received its final finish. The wax is kneaded with the fingers and introduced into the holes with the help of a wooden spatula.

Sanding and Polishing

Preparing the surface for final sanding is just as important as the final finishing itself. We should remember the saying: "A good sanding is half of a good finish." The two processes used to prepare a wood surface for finishing are sanding and polishing.

Sanding can be done with the help of steel wool folded to fit the hand, always rubbing in the direction of the grain of the wood. Cylindrical, rounded, or turned areas are easily sanded with a length of steel wool and twine cut to fit. The twine will help hold the metal fibers and keep the length from coming apart after frequent twisting. It is held at each end and pulled back and forth with both hands, thus sanding the wood with the length of steel wool.

Sandpaper comes in different qualities and grits, allowing us to achieve various finishes and very smooth surfaces. It is a good idea to begin a sanding job with a rough paper and finish it with a finer one. Sandpaper can be used directly, applying pressure with the fingertips (never with the palm of the hand). Always rub in the direction of the grain of the wood, adjusting the pressure of the fingers to the wood's own irregularities. On large, perfectly smooth surfaces a sanding block can be used to hold the paper.

Polishing imparts very fine texture to the wood. It begins with a thorough preliminary sanding of the wood, which is then wet with tap water to raise the grain. Rubbing with the help of a wood block or a piece of cork will remove the raised grain and give a polished look to the wood.

▶ **Steel wool.**

1. Steel wool usually comes in rolls or spools. Because of the natural characteristics of the material (continuous steel filaments), it is a good idea to cut it with scissors after pulling it tight at the point it is to be cut off. This way you will make a clean cut without injuring your hands.

◀ **2.** To work with steel wool, fold the piece in three parts by making two folds. The result is a rectangular-shaped surface the size of a hand.

▼ **Steel wool braid.**

1. A steel wool braid helps strip and sand difficult-to-reach corners. A large piece of steel wool and a piece of thick twine twice as long as the steel wool are needed to make it. The twine will keep the steel wool from fraying.

▼ **2.** Lay the twine along both sides of the steel wool. Hold the ends of the twine and the steel wool in one hand while twisting the opposite ends with the other hand, until a very tight spiral is made.

▲ **3.** Once the spiral is tightly wound, fold it in half and twist again. This creates a braid that will stay wound and not unravel.

▶ **4.** The braid works well for sanding round surfaces or turned parts like rings, legs, splats... In this case, we are stripping some turned furniture legs.

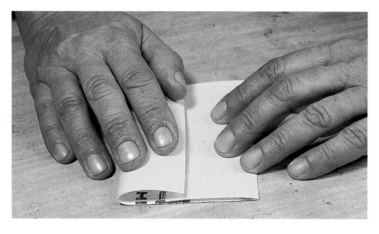

▲ **Sandpaper.**

1. To work with sandpaper, cut a rectangular piece slightly larger than the hand. Then make two folds so that one side overlaps the other between $1/4$ and $1/2$ inch ($1/2$ to 1 cm). This way the upper layer stays put and the folded piece stays firm and easy to work with.

◀ **3.** A wood block can help the work of sanding a completely even surface. It is wrapped with a piece of sandpaper, which is firmly held to the block with the thumb on one side and the fingers on the other; the block is guided with the index finger.

▲ **2.** The sanding motion should always be lengthwise, in the direction of the grain. The pressure on the paper, and therefore on the wood should be applied with the fingertips (not with the palm of the hand), in such a way that the paper and the fingers move in unison over the wood, resulting in a good sanded finish. Antique boards are rarely even, but by varying the pressure of the fingers you can perfectly smooth the surface.

◀ Polishing.

1. The polishing process begins with a thorough sanding (two consecutive sandings with 100 grit and 150 grit sandpapers) and then wetting the wood. It can be moistened with a cotton rag and tap water. This application will raise the grain of the wood.

▼ 2. A wood block with a cork is used to polish the wood. Pieces of cork cut to fit can be used around moldings, corners, and hard-to-reach areas. In some areas with very tight corners a soft, natural fiber brush can be used.

▼ 3. When the wood is completely dry, the surface should be vigorously rubbed with the cork. This will remove the raised grain from the surface and result in a deeply burnished wood finish.

The final finishes applied to wood are wax, lacquer, and varnish. It is important not to forget that the period and the style of the furniture will dictate which is used. The best and most valuable piece of period furniture can lose all its value and charm if it is given an inappropriate finish. If the object to be restored had a wax or lacquered finish at the time it was made, another different finish should never be applied; to do so would be to falsify one of the most visible characteristics of the object. Practical criteria should never prevail over the original finish.

Wax

Wax is the most common and most antique finish. It is applied to the surface of the wood and, once dry, shined by buffing with a wool or cotton lint-free cloth. There are prepared waxes of different qualities, consistencies, and colors that can be applied directly to the wood. It is also possible to make wax finish in the shop. Use 8 ounces (200 g) of pure beeswax, 8 ounces (200 g) of paraffin (adds consistency and keeps the cost down), 8 ounces (200 g) of carnuba wax flakes (adds hardness), and one quart (1 liter) of good quality turpentine. The solid ingredients are melted in a double boiler until a smooth paste is formed. Remove the paste from the heat source and add the turpentine and coloring agents (asphaltum, colored pigments, or universal tints) if a colored wax is desired. It can be stored in a covered metal container to prevent the evaporation of the turpentine. If a more liquid wax is needed, part of this wax can be melted in a double boiler and turpentine added until reaching the desired consistency.

◀ **Making and applying wax.**
1. Making furniture wax in the shop is a simple process. Begin by preparing your materials (pure beeswax, paraffin, carnuba, and color, if necessary) and the utensils (hammer and chisel, scales, hotplate, small handled pot, metal container with a lid, and a wood spatula). The first step consists of chipping small pieces from the block of pure beeswax with the help of the hammer and chisel.

◀ **2.** The pieces of beeswax must be as small as possible, so they will melt quickly with the rest of the components of the mixture. Then a similar quantity of chips is cut from the block of paraffin.

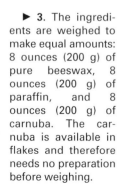

▶ **3.** The ingredients are weighed to make equal amounts: 8 ounces (200 g) of pure beeswax, 8 ounces (200 g) of paraffin, and 8 ounces (200 g) of carnuba. The carnuba is available in flakes and therefore needs no preparation before weighing.

▲ **4.** The three ingredients are mixed in a small pot and heated in a double boiler. Stir the mixture with a wood spatula until all the materials are completely melted.

▲ **5.** When a smooth paste is achieved, remove the pot and let it cool slightly. Add a quart (1 liter) of turpentine to the still warm mixture while stirring with the spatula. If the wax requires a different tone, asphaltum or colorants can be added as needed.

▲ **6.** Finish the process by pouring the warm wax into a metal container with a wide mouth for ease of use. The container should always be kept closed to prevent the evaporation of the turpentine, which would cause the wax to lose plasticity.

▶ **7.** The wax can be applied with the help of a cotton pad or directly by hand. It should be applied in thin layers, always applying the last one in the direction of the grain.

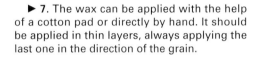

▼ **8.** Polishing the waxed surface is done by vigorously buffing with a clean cotton or wool rag. Used and recycled rags work very well, because they do not leave any lint stuck to the surface.

▼ **9.** Polish curved, turned, or carved surfaces using small strips of rag, using both hands in a continuous back and forth movement.

Shellac and Varnish

Shellac is another commonly used finish. There are different kinds of shellac on the market that are ready to use. Preparation in the shop is fast and simple. Shellac is a product that comes in flakes, is sold by weight, and can be found with different colorations. Eight ounces (200 g) of shellac and one quart (1 liter) of alcohol are needed. The mixture is placed in a bottle and shaken until the flakes are completely dissolved. Different concentrations can be made for different uses (a thick shellac is appropriate for rustic style furniture). Shellac is a natural substance, made from the secretions of the lac insect which lives in different kinds of trees in India and Thailand, and is the only resin of animal origin. For this reason, there will always be a certain amount of impurities, which will have to be removed before its application. The most common methods of application are with a rag or a finishing pad; it is only applied with a brush on certain occasions. Applying shellac with a pad is difficult, laborious, and requires a controlled environment. It gives a finish that equally highlights the beauty and the defects (if there are any) of the wood; nevertheless, it is a high-quality finish. It is applied in a room with low humidity, with a temperature between 60 and 65°F (15 and 18°C) in a dust- and particle-free environment, and with indirect lighting in the work area. The first step is to charge the pad with more alcohol than shellac and then to spread it over the surface of the wood, making overlapping figure eights.

Gradually the concentration of alcohol diminishes and the shellac increases; at the same time, the size of the overlapping figure eight motions increases to large sweeping movements in the direction of the wood grain over the entire surface. Finally, the shellac is applied back and forth along the grain of the wood. With each application the cloth that covers the pad is turned, to avoid the crusting and thickening of material that could cause streaks. It is important to charge the rubbing pad when it begins to stick to the surface or when it is not "moistening," that is to say, when we do not see the fumes. An excessive charge can cause the characteristic ripples, the appearance of thickened shellac in the form of hills or ridges, resulting from a heavy application that was worked too little (not spread enough).

Varnish is a finish that is not used very much in restoration. The most useful kind of varnish is nitrocellulose, a pore-filling type for rustic-style finishes. It is applied using a rag or a pad, and it is sanded with 400 grit silicon-carbide paper to remove possible roughness. A final pass with fine steel wool (number 0000) will remove the sanding marks.

▲ Preparing and applying shellac.
1. Begin the shellac mixing process by preparing the necessary materials: shellac flakes, alcohol 96°, a scale, a glass container with an airtight lid, a plastic bottle with a very small opening, a funnel, and a very fine-weave cloth or a length of panty hose. The shellac flakes are weighed and mixed in a proportion of 8 ounces (200 g) for each quart (1 liter) of alcohol.

◄ 2. Put the shellac into the glass bottle, and add the alcohol to it; then cap the bottle to prevent evaporation.

▲ 3. Leave the mixture in the bottle until the shellac has completely dissolved. Shaking the bottle from time to time will help. It is important to close the lid tightly to prevent evaporation of the alcohol and possible leaks or splashing when the bottle is shaken.

▶ 4. Shellac is a natural product and always has a certain amount of impurities, which must be removed before it can be used. To do so, we filter the mixture by pouring it through a funnel (placed in a plastic bottle) in which we have placed a finely woven piece of cloth or a length of panty hose. This way we get a mixture free of impurities in a bottle with a narrow mouth, which will make it easy to dispense.

▼ 5. A finishing pad can be used for applying shellac. To make one, a small quantity of clean cotton or wool strands or cheesecloth is needed along with a piece of cotton fabric. The fabric must have been used (perhaps rags made of old clothing) or washed, to eliminate any sizing. The first step is to make a tight ball of the strands or cloth the size of your hand. Then pound one side of the ball to create a flat and compressed surface.

▼ 6. Cover the flat surface of the ball with a square piece of the fabric, so that it is perfectly centered. Gather the four corners of the square behind the pad.

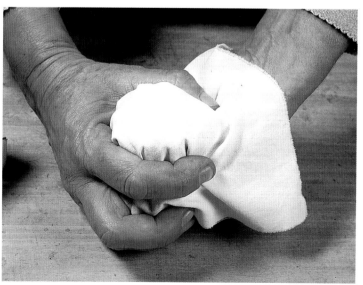

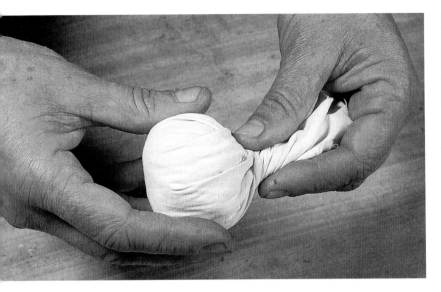

▲ **7.** Holding the ball with one hand, twist the four corners so that they stay together to form a handle.

▲ **8.** The correct way to hold the rubbing pad to apply shellac is to place the handle under the little finger and the ring finger against the palm of the hand and spread the thumb, index, and middle fingers in a tripod shape to hold the sides of the pad.

◄ **9.** The pad is charged by pouring a generous amount of shellac directly onto the ball without the fabric.

▼ **11.** Cover the ball with the fabric and lightly tap the surface until it is completely soaked. Before beginning to apply the shellac, add two drops of liquid Vaseline to act as a lubricant.

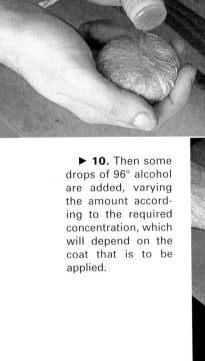

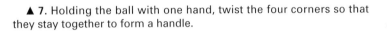

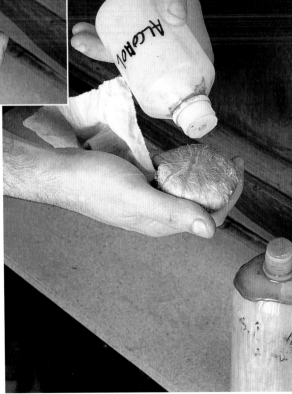

► **10.** Then some drops of 96° alcohol are added, varying the amount according to the required concentration, which will depend on the coat that is to be applied.

► **12.** The shellac is applied to the surface of the wood with a figure eight motion, charging the pad whenever it sticks too much or the alcohol no longer evaporates. The outside cloth is charged with each application, and the pad should be kept in a sealed container after use.

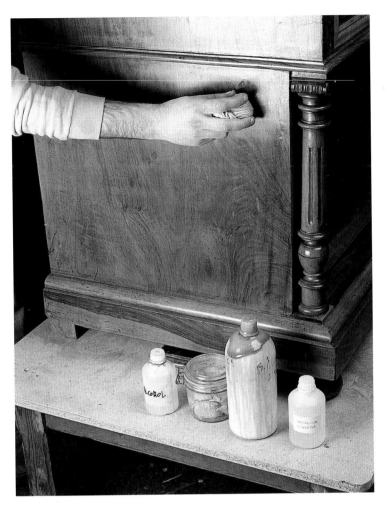

Other Finishes

There are other kinds of finishes that are combinations of the previous ones and that give different kinds of results.

The **mechado** is a finish with a warm, satiny quality that is very appropriate for rustic-style oak furniture. It is done by applying several coats of wax until the pores are completely filled, and then buffing with a soft, natural fiber brush. Next, two or three coats of shellac are applied, and once dried it is covered with a last coat of wax. It is burnished by rubbing with the brush and then buffing it with a cotton or wool cloth.

French polishing imparts a high-quality glossy finish that highlights the natural beauty of the wood, and also its imperfections, acting as a magnifying mirror for the quality and defects. The process begins with an application of shellac with cheesecloth to fill the pores of the wood, and then a sprinkling of pumice (finely ground) over the surface being treated. Using an alcohol-charged finishing pad, wipe with the same motions as when applying shellac, until a paste forms that will penetrate the wood from the pressure of the hand. After 24 hours, finish the surface with a coat of shellac.

The **filler and wax** finish is surely the most widely used in restoration. The filler is applied with cotton strands or a rag until the pores are completely filled, and finished with a pad. When it is completely dry, the surface is sanded with silicon carbide paper and a fine (number 0000) steel wool. Finally, a coat of wax is applied and polished with a cotton or wool cloth.

An **encaustic** finish is achieved by supersaturating the wood with wax to achieve a high gloss. Hot liquid wax is applied with rags or a brush onto the surface of the wood. The wax can be buffed when it is cold and has solidified.

The **relleno de cera** (derived from the French *ciré remplie*) consists of waxing the surface of the wood, sprinkling it with pumice, and rubbing in the resulting paste in circular motions with a pad charged with alcohol on the inside and wax on the outside. Pressure on the pad causes the pumice paste to penetrate the wood. The last pass always must go in the direction of the wood grain.

▼ **13.** The application of shellac begins with small figure eight motions with a pad charged with a little shellac and a greater amount of alcohol (A). As more coats are applied, the amount of alcohol decreases and the shellac increases, while the figure eight motions become larger (B). End with large zigzag motions (C), and apply the last coat wiping in the direction of the wood grain (D).

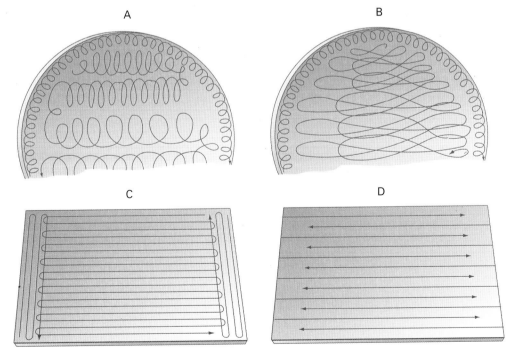

A

B

C

D

Furniture Assembly

The last step in the restoration process consists of reassembling the accessories once they have been cleaned, retouching small imperfections, and a general cleaning of the entire object.

Cleaning and Assembling Parts

The last concern before reassembling a piece of furniture is cleanliness. A part should never be reattached without first having been cleaned. Dirty marble, glass, or metal parts undermine the whole restoration process.

Marble can be cleaned with special commercial products or with oxalic acid that is rinsed with water. A thorough waxing and buffing is required, to give it a very natural look, before proceeding to attach the piece.

Metal parts should be cleaned with an appropriate commercial product, rubbing with a piece of steel wool or a wire brush to reach the smallest crevices. Finally, buff by rubbing with a cotton cloth.

Glass can also be cleaned with a commercial product, or if there are stains on the surface, they can be removed with a scraper or blade.

After cleaning and polishing, the parts should be reattached in the same order they were removed, following the sketches and marks made at that time.

▲ **Cleaning marble.**
1. The marble top of a washstand is cleaned with a special commercially available product for cleaning marble. The surface is lightly polished by wiping the product and removing it with cotton strands or a rag dipped in water.

▼ **2.** To impart a natural shine to the marble that will not clash with the restoration of the whole piece of furniture, it is polished with furniture wax. When dry, it is buffed with a fine cotton rag.

▲ Cleaning a metal part.

1. The metal parts from a dresser drawer are cleaned by applying a commercial metal cleaning product, using a small piece of steel wool so that the paste penetrates all the detailed areas.

▲ 2. Since this is a part with a lot of detail, it is necessary to keep brushing with a soft wire brush (a brush for cleaning suede) in some areas, to completely eliminate the dirt.

▲ 3. When it is completely clean, polish it with a cotton cloth to remove any possible traces of metal cleaner and to get the desired shine.

▶ 4. Once the parts have been cleaned and polished, they are reattached in the same order in which they were removed, according to the sketch or notes that were made at the time or the marks made during the process. This way they will work as well as they did before the restoration process.

Retouching

Sometimes a final retouching of color is necessary before completing the project. This helps hide small discolored areas that were left from the beginning, because of their minor importance, or that have appeared during some phase of the restoration process. Usually a commercial stain is applied with a photo retouching brush or directly with markers. In both cases, the application is blended by lightly tapping the surface with a finger, to spread it evenly. In certain cases, minor retouching can be done with a brush and shellac tinted with alcohol-soluble aniline dyes.

◄ Retouching with a brush.
1. To complete the last color touch-up, an alcohol-based color can be used. It will not raise the wood grain and stands up well to light. It is applied with a sable photo retouching brush.

◄ 2. To hide the retouching and blend the color with the rest of the wood, spread by lightly tapping it with the finger before the alcohol evaporates.

▼ Retouching with markers.
1. Retouching markers can be used to correct minor color defects, even over a coat of varnish. The desired color is applied directly with the marker.

▼ 2. The color is smoothed by tapping with the finger until it is totally blended into the wood's surface.

Interior and Exterior Cleaning

A restoration project ends with a light cleaning of the interior of the furniture piece: drawers, shelves, bottoms... Alcohol is customarily used for general cleaning, and scrapers and steel wool are used in areas that require more effort because of the presence of stains or layers of dirt.

A final vacuuming inside and out with a powerful vacuum cleaner, with various attachments, will remove any traces of dirt or particles from the piece.

▲ **1.** Certain elements, like drawers, have a tendency to accumulate grime and dirt that must be removed; otherwise it will diminish even the best restoration project. One way to clean them is to remove the layer of dirt with scrapers.

◄ **3.** If there are no stained or very dirty areas, a general cleaning of the whole interior is carried out using rags soaked in alcohol. Finish by applying coats of filler and wax.

► **2.** If there are stains or a great amount of dirt, it will be necessary to begin the cleaning using a scraper, and then rub the surfaces vigorously with steel wool soaked with alcohol. Cleanup is completed by removing residual dirt with a rag soaked in alcohol.

► **4.** The project ends with a thorough vacuuming of the interior and the exterior, to impart a tidiness to the restored piece.

*T*he exercises in this chapter have been chosen and arranged according to their level of difficulty from less to more by the main process used in each project. In the first of these, involving the Thonet-style rocking chair, the main theme will be the total disassembly of the chair and the blending of the color and tone of all the pieces. In the section on the rustic table, the stripping process and simple carpentry repairs are explained. For the rustic trunk that is in poor condition, simple reinforcing pieces are constructed for the frame of the trunk. The exercise based on the Isabelline-style chair deals with the disassembly process and then the gluing of the fairly complicated assemblies, and shows how to make complex reinforcing parts. The process of restoring the Isabelline-style sewing table includes the repair of an area with missing veneer. Various processes are explained in the restoration of the eighteenth-century chest of drawers: replacing inlay work, reinforcing different parts of the frame of a piece of furniture, and making a new part. The section on the mirror represents an example of furniture constructed with parts of other furniture pieces that will be given new value by gilding. The restoration of the chest covers the steps for repairing pieces of marquetry work and making a part with resin. Finally, the work on the Modernist-style wardrobe emphasizes the final finish of the wood. In addition to the central themes, all of the exercises explain complete restoration processes that demonstrate solutions and above all various finishes that are special and unique to each case.

Step by *Step*

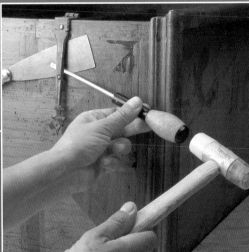

Thonet-Style Rocking Chair

*S*ometimes a piece that has been previously restored must be restored again. It is possible that the first restoration was not done well, because poor quality materials were used or recommended practices were not followed, or perhaps the piece has later suffered deterioration due to use or poor treatment. A bad restoration job can considerably shorten the useful life of an object.

In this case, we are dealing with a rocking chair with a strong frame but that requires various repairs. These consist of undoing old restorations, totally disassembling the chair, strengthening some parts, and applying an appropriate finish to the wood; this last step is the one that will give new value to the rocking chair. The filling and assembly of the parts will permit the daily use for which the chair was manufactured.

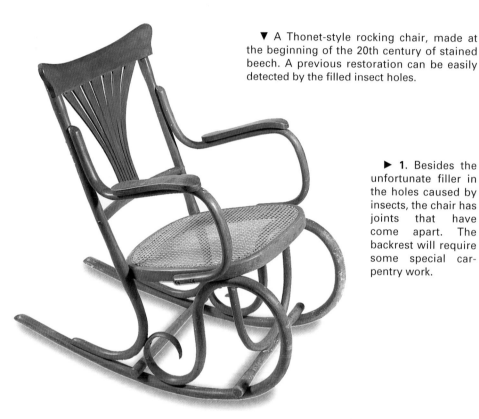

▼ A Thonet-style rocking chair, made at the beginning of the 20th century of stained beech. A previous restoration can be easily detected by the filled insect holes.

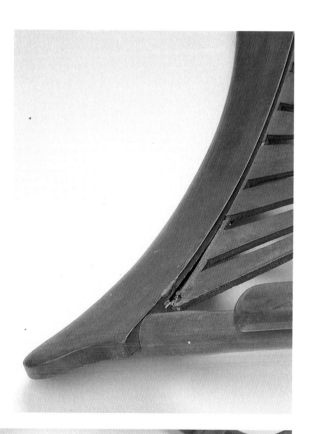

▶ **1.** Besides the unfortunate filler in the holes caused by insects, the chair has joints that have come apart. The backrest will require some special carpentry work.

▶ **2.** Different areas of the rocker show wood that has been cracked and discolored by use. The color differences, easily noticed, make the chair ugly, reduce its value, and give it an air of decrepitude.

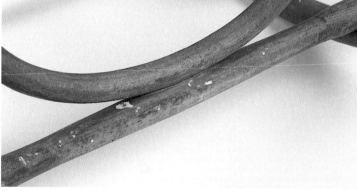

▲ **3.** A thorough examination of the filled holes shows that all are intact and that there are no holes without filler. Because of this, and after a minute examination of all parts of the rocking chair, including the underside and less visible areas, we arrive at the conclusion that the insects are no longer active. It will not be necessary to apply an insecticide.

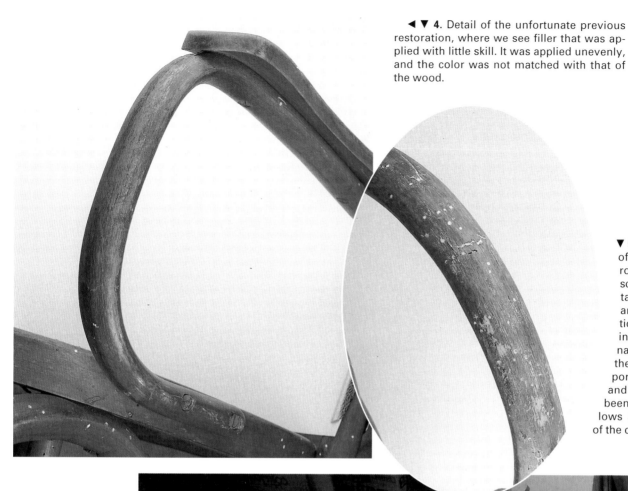

◄ ▼ **4.** Detail of the unfortunate previous restoration, where we see filler that was applied with little skill. It was applied unevenly, and the color was not matched with that of the wood.

▼ **5.** The first step consists of dismantling the entire rocker. Each part is unscrewed in order, and detailed notes or sketches are made of their location as this is being done, including the kinds of nails and screws that hold the parts together. It is important to keep the sketch and the screws that have been listed, because this allows a quick final assembly of the chair.

▲ **6.** The caning on the seat is protected with masking tape. It has to be applied very carefully, since it must protect the caning from the stripping and sanding of the seat frame to which it is attached.

▲ **7.** To begin the stripping process, it is necessary to scrub the surface with a rag soaked in alcohol. This procedure softens both the old varnish and the filler.

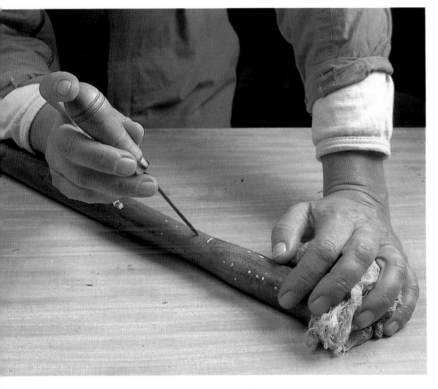

▲ **8.** To remove the old filler, now softened, an awl is used. It is pushed into the hole to extract the filler.

► **9.** When all of the filler has been removed, all of the pieces are rubbed with steel wool to remove any small traces of varnish.

▲ **10.** Once all of the parts of the rocker have been thoroughly stripped, they can be sanded. To start off, they are sanded with a medium grit sandpaper (100 grit) to remove most of the stain, changing to a fine paper (150 grit) to get a smooth surface.

The arm at the right side of the photograph shows the color of the stain on the wood before sanding.

▲ **11.** Notable differences in coloration as a result of heavy use can be seen on different parts of this rocker. Some areas have more color than others, resulting in unattractive stains. To even out the color of the different pieces, they are bleached. A super-saturated solution of oxalic acid in water is applied with a brush.

◄ **12.** When the part is dry, the oxalic acid solution is removed by washing it with a rag and a lot of water.

► **13.** When the wood has dried, it is a good idea to sand it with a fine paper (150 grit, for example), to remove any grain that has been raised.

◀ ▲ 14. Finally, to completely even out the overall color of the chair, a coat of stain (aniline dye dissolved in water) is applied with a brush.

▲ 15. While the recently applied stain is still damp, drips are removed by drying them with a cotton rag. By doing this, we make sure that the color will be even and without streaks.

▶ 16. The water in the dye has raised the grain. Sandpaper cannot be used to remove it, because the recently applied color will disappear. So once the wood is dry, it is rubbed with a soft natural fiber brush until the raised grain is completely eliminated, leaving a smooth surface. (Europeans often use esparto grass, which is not readily available in the United States.)

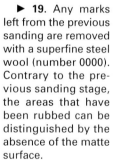

◄ **17.** The next step consists of filling the pores of the wood to begin the final finishing. Using cotton strands or a rag, a commercial filler is applied in very light coats. These have to be light so that they dry quickly after they are applied, permitting the immediate application of one coat after another on the same part.

▲ **18.** We then proceed with the final sanding to create a completely smooth surface. This is done with wet paper (number 400). The sanded area has a matte look compared with the shiny areas resulting from the application of the filler. It is important not to remove this matte finish, since it shows the areas that have been sanded and those that have not, and it will help speed up the project.

► **19.** Any marks left from the previous sanding are removed with a superfine steel wool (number 0000). Contrary to the previous sanding stage, the areas that have been rubbed can be distinguished by the absence of the matte surface.

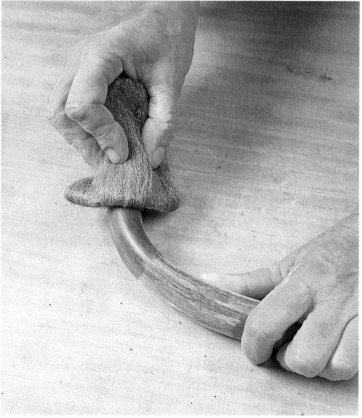

► **20.** The cracks and holes caused by the action of insects are filled by applying hard wax with a spatula. The great variety of colors, textures, and brands of these waxes allows us to choose a tone to match the color of the wood.

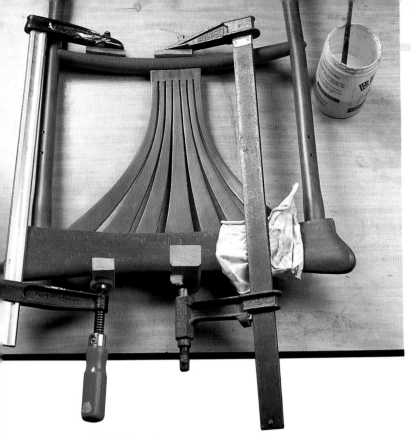

▲ **21.** Parts that require it are joined and glued before waxing and assembling the chair. In this case, two parts of the backrest have been joined using common white glue and are held with clamps.

▲ **22.** Finally, all the parts of the rocker are waxed with fine furniture wax.

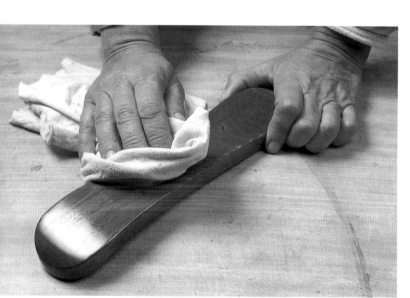

▲ **23.** When the wax is dry, it is vigorously polished with a clean cotton rag until the desired shine is achieved.

▶ **24.** The rocking chair is then reassembled, referring to the sketches or notes made during the disassembly stage.

◄ 25. If necessary, a final color touch-up in small areas can be done using a sable photo retouching brush.

► 26. The final result is a sturdy and attractive rocking chair.

Rustic Drop Leaf Table

*S*ometimes an appropriate treatment will transform an old piece (of little value) into a useful piece with great aesthetic value. The goal of restoration is to return the usefulness and lost beauty of an object. The restoration process can also create new value in an object.

In this case, a fairly simple restoration has revitalized a nearly useless table that had been very roughly treated in its daily use.

The table, constructed of pine, is rustic in style, notable for the simplicity of its forms; it has a top with two drop leaves, and was made to be very serviceable in its day-to-day use in a work environment. Because of this, we are faced with the restoration of a battered and abused object.

▲ One of the drop leaves is broken at a place near the tabletop. Such a break was surely caused from forcing it opened or closed.

▲ During an exhaustive inspection of the table, we learn that the fixed tabletop and the two drop leaves are the most damaged parts. We note the presence of several stains made by different kinds of paint (some quite old) and broken and disjointed parts.

▶ The fixed tabletop is made of boards joined together, and one of them has come apart. In addition to the many paint stains, we note the presence of pitting on the surface of the wood.

▶ **1.** The first step in this project will be to strip the table to remove all of the paint stains. To do this, we will apply caustic soda, since solid pine can withstand such aggressive treatment. It is important to keep in mind that caustic soda is a chemical irritant and poses a certain level of danger. Therefore, when using it, it will be necessary to wear a respirator for fumes, long neoprene gloves, safety glasses, and heavy clothing to protect all parts of the body. It is also recommended that it be used in a secure place with few people around, outdoors if possible, or at least in a well-ventilated place.

We prepare a solution of caustic soda: In a bucket of hot water we dilute 2 pounds (1 kg) of caustic soda in 1 gallon (5 liters) of water, stirring it until completely diluted. Near this, we place another bucket of clear water.

▶ **3.** Always holding the hands in a downward, vertical position (to prevent the possibility of unpleasant effects from dripping), we wring the rag over the surface that we wish to treat until it is entirely soaked in the solution.

▲ **2.** Well-protected, we soak a cotton rag in the soda solution. The rag should not have hanging threads, to avoid splashing.

▶ **4.** With the cotton rag, we spread the solution evenly over the whole surface we wish to strip.

▲ 5. We soak another rag in the clean water that we had set aside.

▼ 7. Using a cabinet scraper, and always in the direction of the wood grain, we scrape the surface of the table until we have totally removed the stains and traces of paint not removed by the caustic soda.

▲ 6. With one hand, we wipe off the soda using the soaked rag, always following the grain of the wood; with the other hand, we sand the wood with steel wool (number 00) to remove the top layer of paint.

After we are finished with the steel wool, we use the rag to begin to rinse the wood with clean water as many times as needed and changing the water often.

◄ 8. Once the wood is completely dry, we begin the woodworking stage to repair the top. We clean the crack where the boards have come apart, using a saw blade to scrape it. Use the blade to eliminate completely all traces of the old glue, so that a perfect bond can be achieved with the new glue.

◄ 9. We protect the two sides of the space from drips with masking tape. To glue such a narrow gap, we apply white glue with a syringe, which will help it to penetrate efficiently and evenly.

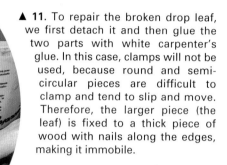

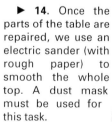

▲ **10.** We hold the pieces we are gluing together with clamps. Wood pieces are placed between the clamps and the object to protect the wood from possible dents. The clamps are placed perpendicular to the pieces that are being glued, and will apply the force needed for the bond. Other clamps are placed at each end of the tabletop; this way, with the help of the wood pieces, they apply vertical force so that one of the two boards being glued does not end up higher than the other. We let the glue dry for 24 hours.

▲ **11.** To repair the broken drop leaf, we first detach it and then glue the two parts with white carpenter's glue. In this case, clamps will not be used, because round and semi-circular pieces are difficult to clamp and tend to slip and move. Therefore, the larger piece (the leaf) is fixed to a thick piece of wood with nails along the edges, making it immobile.

▶ **12.** We glue the surface of each of the pieces using a brush and white carpenter's glue.

▶ **14.** Once the parts of the table are repaired, we use an electric sander (with rough paper) to smooth the whole top. A dust mask must be used for this task.

▲ **13.** The smaller piece is also held in place with nails driven into the thick wood base. Use as many nails as necessary to hold the piece, so that it asserts enough pressure to achieve a good bond.

◄ **15**. A second hand sanding with fine sandpaper is needed to remove the circular marks caused by the electric sander.

▼ **16**. The finishing of the table begins with an application of filler with cotton strands or a rag. It is applied in the direction of the wood grain, continuing until the pores are completely filled. Filler is always applied in thin coats, which dry rapidly and allow immediate additional coats.

▼ **17**. Once the filler has dried, a final sanding is done to achieve a completely smooth surface. This is done with wet sandpaper (400 grit), always in the direction of the grain, rubbing until the surface is smooth to the touch.

► **18**. The final finish consists of applying wax to all surfaces of the wood and rubbing vigorously with a cotton cloth until the desired gloss is achieved. If needed, we can apply several coats of wax, buffing it afterward to get a richer, deeper finish.

◀ **19.** The result is a table with an attractive honey color whose usefulness has been restored.

Rustic Trunk

*S*ometimes restoring an object means giving it a new look and, therefore, new value. Some furniture was partially or entirely lined with covering considered to be of the richest kind, usually fabric or leather. Because of their fragility, these coverings have suffered a lot of damage, and in many cases have disappeared almost completely.

One of the premises of restoration is the conservation whenever possible of all the original elements, but in some cases it is important to decide which is the most appropriate approach: the conservation, elimination, or changing of the original material. One guideline that should be followed is to maintain the usefulness of the object and conserve the parts if they do not hinder its use and aesthetic enjoyment.

▼ A very plain trunk, which was covered on the outside with fabric held in place by nails that are still there. Because it was covered on the outside, the original finish of the wood was extremely rough.

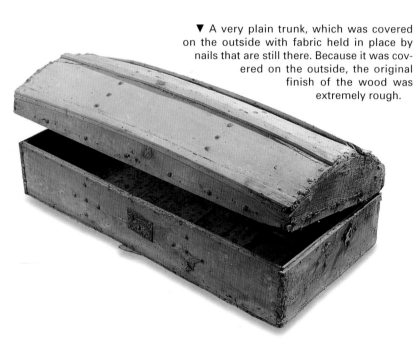

▲ The interior of the chest was lined with printed paper.

► One end still has the leather handle and much of the original fabric. Since it is impossible to conserve the original fabric and handle, the entire exterior covering of the chest will be removed.

▲ Because it was made of a very soft wood that encouraged insect attacks, large areas of material have been lost. The reinforcement on the top has almost completely disappeared.

► The opposite end is missing the handle. It shows a lot of wear and tear and loss of material through the action of parasites.

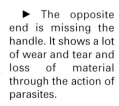

◀ **2.** The loose exterior braces of the chest, and the tongue and grooves between boards that were displaced and laying one over the other are bonded with white glue. The parts are held in place with clamps and allowed to dry for 24 hours.

▲ **1.** Active wood-boring insects have been detected in the wood. An insecticide will be applied on the exterior and interior with a brush. Neoprene gloves and a respirator for fumes should be used. The paper has been easily removed to allow total impregnation of the wood.

▶ **3.** The supports at the bottom of the chest suffered great loss of material and areas of rot. Therefore, the frame and cross supports are removed using a lifter and pincers.

▼ **4.** Pieces similar in length and width are cut and bonded to the bottom of the chest with white glue. The pieces forming the frame are glued on first, and then the inside crosspieces.

▼ **5.** To secure and reinforce the wood pieces, we attach them with special staple brads. We will countersink them using a nail set and a hammer.

◄ **6.** The wood in this piece had never been finished, because it was covered with fabric and would not have been seen. The whole surface is cleaned with a rough steel wool to remove dust and grime.

▲ **7.** Wood pieces similar to those that are missing are cut and dampened, to aid in slightly bending and forming them to the top of the chest. We spread white glue on them and attach them for 24 hours with tourniquets (in the bowed area), in addition to two clamps at the ends to hold the flat areas and to hold the chest to the workbench.

◄ **8.** A rasp is used on the ends of the new braces to break the sharp edges and round the ends of the wood pieces.

► **9.** The paper that covered the interior of the trunk is removed. Hot water is applied to the paper with a rag while scraping with a spatula.

▼ **10.** Since the old wood is very dry (it has never been given a finish), we revive it with a couple of coats of raw linseed oil mixed in equal portions with a drying agent on the entire surface, except on the new pieces of wood. The linseed oil deepens the tone of the wood.

► **11.** Once the linseed oil has dried, the original color of the wood can be seen. We will stain the new pieces the same color with an aniline dye dissolved in water and applied with a brush.

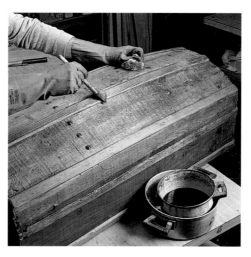

▲ **13.** Encaustic, a rustic finish in keeping with the piece, is applied. Solid finishing wax is liquefied in a double boiler and applied to the wood with a brush while it is still hot. This is done as often as necessary until the wood is completely impregnated with wax.

▲ **12.** The wood on the inside of the trunk will be protected with a coat of nitrocellulose filler, applied with a rag. Neoprene gloves and a respirator with a filter for organic vapors should be used during the whole process.

▶ **14.** After adding new leather handles of a color that does not clash with that of the wood, the trunk is polished, buffing it with a cotton cloth.

◀ **15.** New value has been given to a rustic piece of poor quality by finishing the wood that had been hidden under a rich covering.

Isabelline-Style Chair

*T*his Isabelline-style chair (second half of the nineteenth century) is made of carved mahogany.

In this case, we are dealing with a high-quality piece with a high market value and much desired by collectors, that has come to the restoration shop in very poor condition. The wood, solid mahogany, and also the style and period in which it was made will influence the type of restoration, which will have to be very respectful of all the characteristics of the piece.

The chair is completely broken; the parts are being held together only by the woven cane seat. Judging by its condition, we deduce that at some point in time it was broken by a very heavy weight that caused several joints to come apart. The restoration process will focus on disassembling the parts to evaluate their condition, repairing and strengthening the pieces of the chair, reinforcing the seat, and a final cleaning to bring back the natural beauty of the mahogany.

▼ All of the parts of the chair were held together by the cane seat. Since it, too, was in poor condition (full of holes) we chose to remove it, in order to evaluate the condition of all the parts of the chair and decide whether to restore them. We find that all of the breaks are very clean and that the missing areas of wood are not a problem.

▲ A rear leg of the chair, where it is joined with dowels to the front part, suffered a vertical break, which then caused the chair to come apart.

▼ The other rear leg suffered only minor splintering, but enough to require that the parts be disassembled. It is interesting to note how the dowels and the triangular reinforcement function as a joint between the curved seat and the straight leg.

▼ An upper frame piece was joined to one of the front legs with a large rectangular tenon, forming a right angle. Being larger and heavier than the rear joints, it was more resistant and therefore separated cleanly, without breaks or splinters.

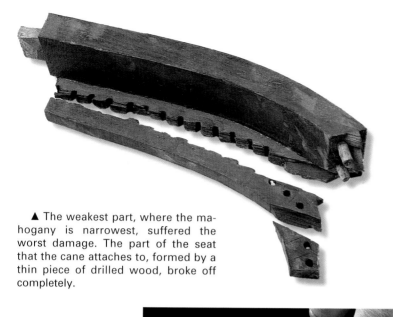

▲ The weakest part, where the mahogany is narrowest, suffered the worst damage. The part of the seat that the cane attaches to, formed by a thin piece of drilled wood, broke off completely.

▲ 1. The first repair consists of removing all traces of the original glue. To do this, we will soften it with hot water and a clean rag.

◄ 2. We remove the softened glue with a chisel. This requires a certain amount of skill, because it is of the utmost importance to damage neither the wood nor the patina on its finish.

▼ 3. We repeat the same process on all of the joints of the chair. This way, when gluing, we will achieve a good bond that will result in a solid structure.

▼ 4. All of the tenons and reinforcing parts have to be completely smooth and clean. We can see the difference after cleaning.

▼ **5.** We can see that the parts that are still together are not as sturdy as we would like and tend to move a little. For this reason, we must take them apart. We clamp the smaller piece to the workbench, protecting the mahogany with wood blocks to keep it from being scratched. We are able to get the pieces apart by striking the larger piece with a mallet (again protecting the mahogany with a wood block).

▲ **6.** Following the same procedure as when we removed the old glue from the dowels, we clean the joint areas. We scrape the glue using a chisel and a nylon mallet until the vertical sides of the mortise are completely clean. The blanket folded at each end protects the curvature of the wood piece and is a simple way to hold it steady.

◀ **7.** Using the chisel, we scrape the residual glue from the corners and bottom of the mortise.

▼ **9.** The parts of the chair are assembled and held together with a tourniquet. This way we can see that no pieces are missing, that all fit together without a problem, and that the assembly is sturdy enough.

◀ **8.** When we removed the leg, it was resistant and left a small broken piece of the square tenon inside the mortise. Because the piece is small and we do not think it will affect the sturdiness of the chair, we do not attempt to remove it. If the break had been large or total, we would have to remove it and make a new tenon.

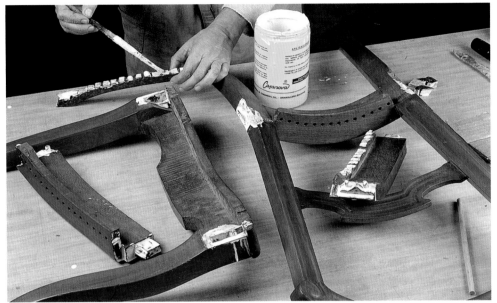

▲ 11. Before clamping the chair to allow the glue to cure well, we have taken the precaution of making some protective pieces for the wood. We seal four rectangular pieces of cardboard with paraffin, and we place one at the corner of each leg, protecting the wood and keeping the glue that oozes out from bonding the cardboard to the wood.

▲ 10. After taking the chair apart, we apply glue to all of the pieces. We use white carpenter's glue and a brush for this step. Glue is applied to both sides of each part, especially in the joints, to the mortise as well as to the tenon.

▶ 12. We hold the legs together with a tourniquet. As it was applied, we saw the need to use clamps to hold other areas, none of which could be allowed to interfere with the rope. For that reason, the tourniquet was placed low. The tourniquet must be thick and strong in order to exert the force needed for a solid bond. Using clamps, we immobilize the small parts that we are going to glue, in this case the seat area. Using a clean rag, we remove the glue that oozes out.

▶ 13. We leave the tourniquet and clamps in place for a minimum of 24 hours to allow the white glue to dry completely. After this time has passed, they can be removed.

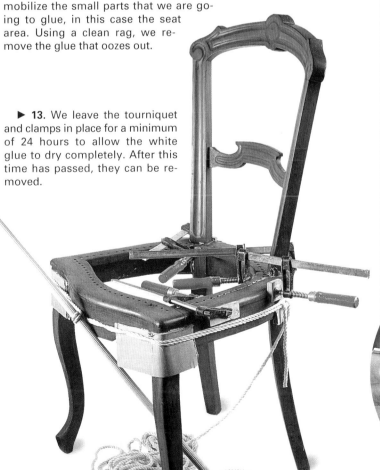

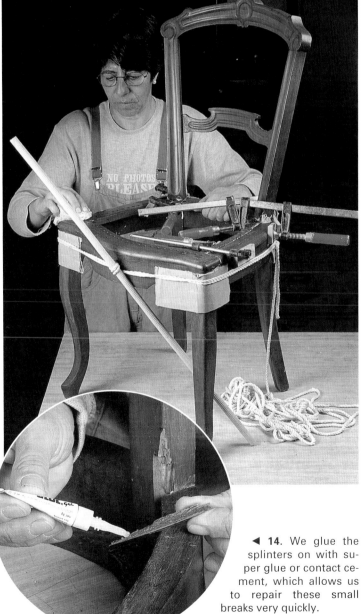

◀ 14. We glue the splinters on with super glue or contact cement, which allows us to repair these small breaks very quickly.

▲ 15. One of the inside areas of the chair is missing a large amount of wood, leaving the dowels visible and making a good joint impossible.

▼ 18. The resin is smoothed and the excess removed using a spatula or chisel before it has totally hardened.

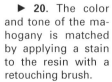

▲ ◄ 16 and 17. A two-part epoxy resin is used to reinforce the area. The parts are mixed following the instructions on the package to make a smooth paste with which we fill the missing area.

◄ 19. Once the resin has completely hardened and cured (it is a fast drying material; the process takes approximately 5 minutes), we sand it even with the wood.

► 20. The color and tone of the mahogany is matched by applying a stain to the resin with a retouching brush.

▼ **21.** To reinforce the parts weakened by the break (the area where the caning was attached) we make two braces, guided by a template of each of them cut out of heavy paper.

▶ **22.** We draw the profile of the template on a board. The board is clamped to the work bench and the pieces cut out using a jigsaw, and the outside edges of each piece are beveled.

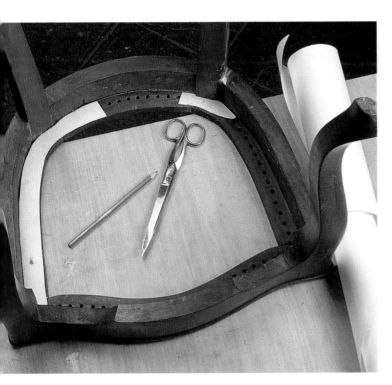

▲ **23.** After staining both pieces, we check their correct fit on the underside of the seat. We also verify that they are beveled enough to hide the supports.

▶ **24.** We apply white carpenter's glue to each of the surfaces that are to be bonded.

◄ 25. The pieces are held in place with clamps, because they have flat surfaces despite their curved profiles. We protect the mahogany on the top of the seat (the most visible area) using wood blocks between it and the clamps.

▼ 26. The underside is not normally visible, so the clamps are used without any protective blocks. We let the glue dry for a minimum of 24 hours.

▼ 27. To attach the caning, it is necessary to drill the new reinforcing pieces that we have made. We use an electric drill with a bit of a slightly smaller diameter than that of the original holes.

◄ 28. Since the general condition of the wood was good, it only needed a thorough cleaning.

We apply a cleaning compound with a rag, later removing the compound with other clean and dry rags.

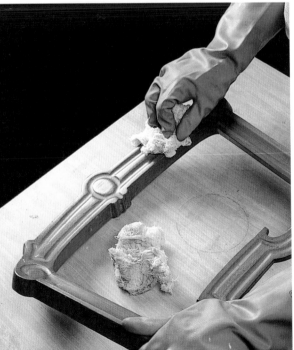

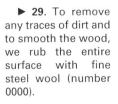

► 29. To remove any traces of dirt and to smooth the wood, we rub the entire surface with fine steel wool (number 0000).

▲ **30**. We apply wax with a rag and polish it by buffing vigorously with a cotton cloth.

▶ **31**. A specialized upholsterer has made the cane seat for the chair. The piece is now ready for the use for which it was made, or to be used as a decorative object.

Isabelline-Style Sewing Table

*T*his sewing table, from the second half of the nineteenth century, is in the Isabelline style and made of pinewood with mahogany veneer.

The piece presents one of the most common problems of veneered furniture: the poor condition (and a missing piece) of the hardwood veneer that covers the frame, which is always made of a common wood. The restoration will necessarily have to focus on replacing it. But the repair can never be an excuse for total replacement of the veneer; doing so would be departing from the premise that the restoration should always be respectful and as minor as possible. Another feature that should be noticed is the tone of the wood. The taste of that period was for dark furniture, and colored varnishes were used to achieve the desired tones. Today the natural mahogany color is preferred; therefore, it will be restored to that tone. For these reasons, the process will center on stripping, repairing the veneer, strengthening the structure, and final finishing of the wood.

◄ The sewing table arrived in poor condition. One look told us that the defects were to be found in the veneer, legs, and crosspieces. We also noticed defects in the coat of varnish that covers it.

► We noted the missing mahogany veneer and some cracking at the corner of the piece.

▼ A set of legs on one side has separated from the body of the table, due to the loss of the nails that held it in place. Because of this, the stretcher has come loose, causing the sewing table to be unstable.

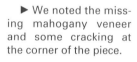

► **1.** The first step consists of removing all of the pulls and locks from the table so they will not be in the way during the different restoration tasks. It is important to make sure that they are correctly marked and stored.

◄ **2.** We disassemble the loose parts, beginning with the legs. Nails normally offer resistance in old furniture pieces. A simple way to help pull them is to strike them with a hammer and a screwdriver, to cause them to move.

► **3.** Once the set of legs is free of nails, we remove the stretcher bar.

Because the stretcher bar is still strongly bonded to the legs, we strike it with a wooden mallet (always using a wooden board for protection) to free it.

► **4.** The area where the stretcher joins the legs has considerable amounts of old glue, which could hinder the bonding of the new glue.

▼ **5.** To avoid the problem, we totally remove the dried glue with a chisel. It is necessary to scrape with care to avoid scratching the wood.

▼ **6.** We apply a commercial stripping product to remove the deteriorated varnish. We always protect our hands and forearms from possible burns by wearing long neoprene gloves.

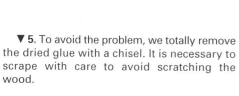

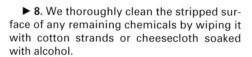

◀ **7.** After enough time has passed to let the chemical work (it differs depending on the brand and the thickness of the coat that has to be removed), we completely remove the stripper with a paint scraper.

▶ **8.** We thoroughly clean the stripped surface of any remaining chemicals by wiping it with cotton strands or cheesecloth soaked with alcohol.

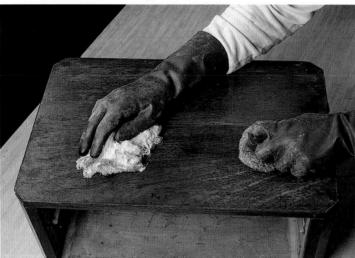

◀ **9.** Once the entire body of the table has been stripped of its varnish, we wipe it with a new alcohol-soaked cotton rag with one hand, in the direction of the wood grain. At the same time, with the other hand, we rub it with number 0000 steel wool.

▼ **10.** We attach the table leg to the workbench with a clamp (always place a wood block in between for protection), and we apply the chemical stripper with a brush.

▲ **11.** In places where it is not possible to use the spatula, as in the case of the turned legs, the chemical stripper is removed with an alcohol-soaked rag.

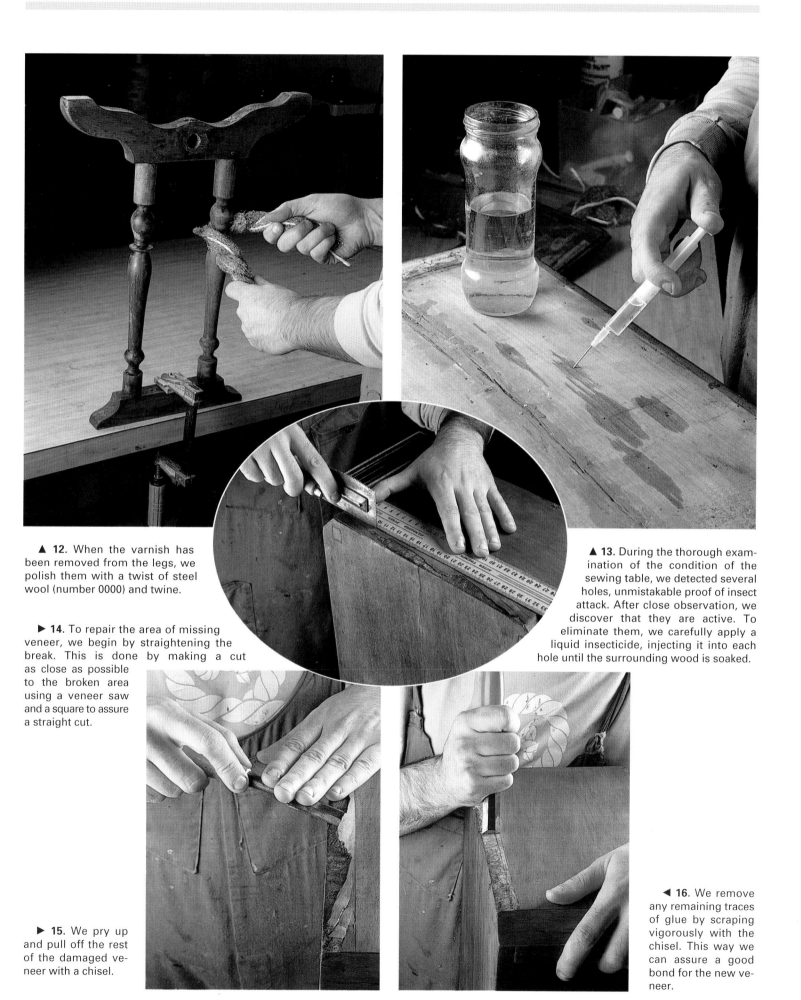

▲ **12.** When the varnish has been removed from the legs, we polish them with a twist of steel wool (number 0000) and twine.

▶ **14.** To repair the area of missing veneer, we begin by straightening the break. This is done by making a cut as close as possible to the broken area using a veneer saw and a square to assure a straight cut.

▲ **13.** During the thorough examination of the condition of the sewing table, we detected several holes, unmistakable proof of insect attack. After close observation, we discover that they are active. To eliminate them, we carefully apply a liquid insecticide, injecting it into each hole until the surrounding wood is soaked.

▶ **15.** We pry up and pull off the rest of the damaged veneer with a chisel.

◀ **16.** We remove any remaining traces of glue by scraping vigorously with the chisel. This way we can assure a good bond for the new veneer.

► **17.** We will attempt to find a veneer that is as close as possible in color and grain to that which we are repairing. Once it is chosen, we cut a piece the same size as the damaged one. This operation is done on a thick wood base, cutting the veneer with a veneer saw so it will not be damaged.

▼ **18.** White carpenter's glue is applied with a brush only on the area to be veneered.

▲ **19.** When the veneer has been placed on the glued area, we apply pressure with a hot iron. This will cause the glue to quickly lose most of the water in its composition, thus activating the bond.

◄ **20.** The new veneer is smoothed and polished using fine sandpaper.

▼ **21.** To even out the color of the wood on different parts of the piece, we use an oxalic acid solution. It is applied with a brush to the entire table. Once dry, the solution is removed by rinsing the wood with generous amounts of water and cotton rags.

◄ **22.** We check to see that we have been able to completely even out the color and tone of the wood.

► **23.** Using a spatula, we fill the cracks, holes caused by the insects, and small defects of the veneer with a commercial mahogany-colored filler.

▲ **24.** We mark with pencil lines the exact area where we have to apply glue for each table leg.

▲ **25.** We apply white carpenter's glue to each piece that is being joined.

◄ **26.** The glued parts are held with clamps for 24 hours. We will remove any dripping glue with clean cotton strands or rags.

▼ **27.** To prepare the table for its final finish, we sand the surface with 150 grit sandpaper in the direction of the wood grain.

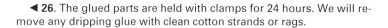

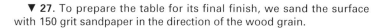

▶ **28.** We vacuum the surface and corners to remove traces of dust. Without such a thorough cleaning, traces of dust from sanding will stick to the wood, spoiling the final finish.

▼ **29.** To achieve a darker mahogany tone, we stain the wood with water-based aniline dye. We apply the solution with a soft rounded brush.

We keep in mind that the aniline will stain, so we protect our hands with long gloves.

▼ **30.** When the surface of the wood is dry, we vigorously rub it with a soft natural fiber brush (or esparto grass) to remove the grain raised by the water.

▼ **31.** To wax the table, we use a powdered wax applied with a rag saturated with paste wax. We spread the wax over the surface using a circular motion. When the coat of wax is dry, the sewing table is polished with a clean cotton rag.

▶ **32.** The final step will add gloss and give depth to the mahogany color. To achieve this, we will apply shellac with lightly soaked cotton rags, always in the direction of the grain of the wood. Finally, we apply a last thin coat of wax, which is then buffed.

▲ **33.** Finally, we reattach the drawer pull and the lock.

The sewing table, now restored, looks very attractive and has a color that is more consistent with today's taste.

Eighteenth-Century Chest of Drawers

*I*n some restoration projects, we are faced with objects that have been modified to a greater or lesser degree. In this case, a very intense evaluation revealed that the proportions of the piece had been modified. The upper and lower parts had been cut down, resulting in a piece that is too low for its width. The changes in the lower part weakened the structure, causing some breakage.

When the proportions were changed, some hardware was moved, namely the pulls. Finally, the surface of the wood was given a rather poor coat of synthetic varnish, which is not appropriate for the period to which the piece belongs, nor to the quality of its wood. We also noted the existence of a problem common to antique furniture with drawers: cracked and broken bottoms caused by the movement of wood that is placed in a longitudinal direction and held between two side pieces.

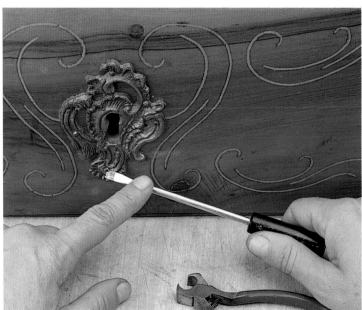

▲ The poor condition of the varnish is best seen on the top surfaces. There are stains from spilled water, humidity, and ink. When the chest of drawers was modified, it was finished with synthetic varnish.

▲ The piece that needs restoring is a Catalan chest of drawers from the 18th century. In the preliminary inspection, we noted that it was constructed of solid walnut with inlaid boxwood strips. Also, it still has the original hardware. There are pieces of wood missing due to rough treatment, missing boxwood inlay in some areas, and numerous cracks as a result of the contraction and movement of the wood.

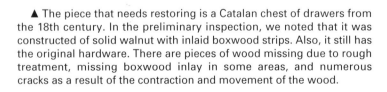

▶ **1.** The first step is to remove the hardware. A screwdriver is used as a lever to pry the nail from the keyhole.

▲ 2. When the nail is loosened, it is pulled out of the escutcheon with pliers. This procedure will not leave marks or scratches on the surface of the wood. All of the furniture hardware should be stored in bags, appropriately numbered and labeled.

▲ 3. The pulls are attached to the drawer fronts with screws. They are loosened by applying drops of lubricating oil on the screws, on both the front and the inside of the drawers, and then using a wrench.

◄ 4. When the pulls have been loosened, they are carefully pulled out by the ends to avoid damaging the wood. We can easily see by the marks on the wood that they were moved from their original positions. The modification of the proportions also affected the pulls, which were centered on the adjusted width of the drawer front but misplaced with respect to the inlaid decoration.

► 5. The wood must be stripped before any other work is done on it. The coat of synthetic varnish will be removed from the entire surface of the chest. Alcohol is applied with clean cotton rags, and the varnish is removed using a steel wool pad. Stripping with alcohol will not damage the wood and decorative inlay work.

▲ **6.** The presence of active wood-boring insects is detected when the drawers are removed. Therefore, an insecticide is used; it is injected into the holes and brushed over the entire surface of the wood.

► **7.** One place that has visible damage is the front corner of a drawer, which is missing a large piece of wood, surely from a blow. A piece of walnut matching the rest of the chest in color and tone is selected to repair it. The piece is clamped to the workbench and planed to the same thickness as that of the drawer front. We check the exact dimensions with calipers.

◄ **8.** The piece is cut using a backsaw and a miter box, so that the angle and the direction of the grain match those of the wood on the drawer front. The area in need of repair has a large knot; therefore, a knotty, heavily grained piece of wood is selected. We try to line up the knot and grain as well as possible to make the new piece blend in.

▼ **9.** The part is glued using carpenter's glue and clamped while it dries. The piece of wood should always be larger than the missing part, so that later it can be cut down to the size and shape of the original.

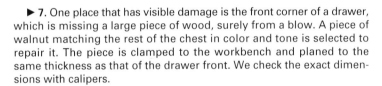

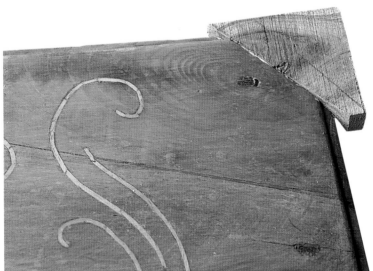

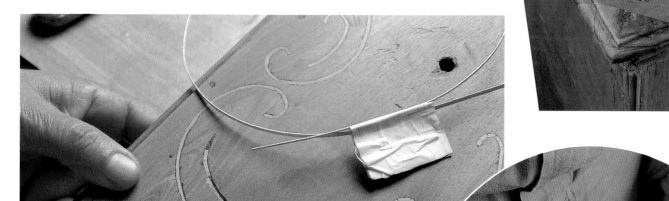

► **10.** The desired shape is achieved using a chisel. A rasp is used to create a rounded corner and curved sides. A final sanding will blend the new piece with the rest of the drawer.

▼ **11.** Some of the inlaid boxwood decorations are missing. The first step in repairing it consists of carefully and thoroughly cleaning the traces of glue and dirt from the inside of the groove in the wood with a scraper.

► **12.** Cut a strip of wood longer than the area that needs repair. This way we can be sure that the whole thing can be repaired with a single piece, avoiding inconsistencies that can mar the result. White PVA glue is applied to the groove in the wood with a fine brush, and the wood strip is placed by applying pressure with a finger.

▼ **13.** We accomplish two things by using a hot iron on the inlay. Pressing with the point helps the strip to completely enter the groove, and the bond is activated by the heat, which speeds up the evaporation of the water in the glue.

► **14.** Next, the leftover piece of the strip is cut off. The part that has remained out of the groove is carefully cut with a sharp blade, while the new piece is held with the fingers to keep it from moving.

▲ 15. While holding down the ends, another pass is made with the hot iron. This finalizes the gluing process and ensures that the points do not stick up. If part of the strip stands out, any sanding, cleaning, or finishing step could cause it to come loose.

▲ 16. The area is wet-sanded with 100 grit sandpaper. The traces of glue are removed and the new piece is brought to the same height as the rest of the boxwood inlay and solid walnut board.

▼ 17. The back part of the chest of drawers has a place where the wood has broken away. The change in the structure of the piece surely caused some areas to be weakened. Bumping or dragging it caused part of the framework to break.

▲ 18. In order to make a repair, the irregular break has to be cut into a regular shape. A square and a pencil are used to lay it out.

◄ **19.** The rectangular shape is carefully cut out with a jigsaw. When this has been done, we discover the existence of an interior brace right at the upper part.

▲ **20.** The brace is slightly lowered with a chisel. This creates a solid support on which to attach the replacement piece.

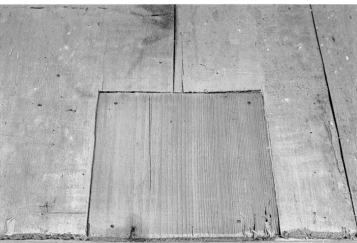

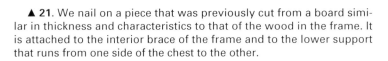

▲ **21.** We nail on a piece that was previously cut from a board similar in thickness and characteristics to that of the wood in the frame. It is attached to the interior brace of the frame and to the lower support that runs from one side of the chest to the other.

► **22.** A common problem in large antique drawers are cracks caused by the expansion and contraction movements of the wood. They are repaired with strips of wood (similar to that of the drawer bottom), which are coated with PVA glue and tapped into place with a nylon-headed hammer. The strips are first shaped with a plane to allow them to fit into the cracks.

▲ 23. It is important that the edges of the strips are flush with the wood on the inside of the drawer bottom. This way the plane will remove only the excess wood on the underside of the drawer, which is always out of sight and does not require a precise finish.

▲ 24. Paper is used to repair small cracks in specific isolated areas. In this case, the bottom outside part of the drawer has been covered with a fragment of old writing paper glued with PVA. The paper reinforces the wood and seals the cracks.

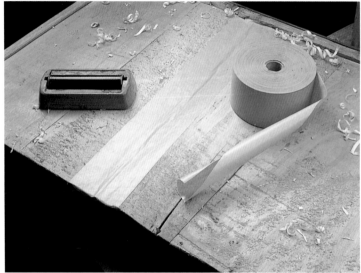

◄ 25. Paper tape is applied to the outside of the drawers to strengthen the breaks repaired with wood strips and to create a more finished look. A roll of paper tape that is wide enough to cover the break is selected and applied wet to the exterior of the drawer bottoms.

▼ 26. The same operation is carried out on the back of the chest of drawers. The paper strengthens the areas between the boards, which are affected by the expansion and contraction movements of the joints.

▼ 27. When the paper tape reinforcements are dry, stain is applied to the back of the piece. A coat of asphaltum is spread using a cotton rag. The overall coloring of the back of the chest will add a dignified and polished aspect to the restoration.

▲ 28. All of the visible surfaces of the chest are sanded by hand: first with a number 100-grit paper and then with a 150-grit paper, always sanding in the direction of the grain of the wood.

► 30. When the surface of the wood has completely dried, it is hand sanded with 220-grit paper. This results in a very smooth, polished wood.

▼ 31. The wetting and sanding process is repeated until a deeply burnished surface is achieved.

▲ 29. To prepare for the final finish and so that the surface will have a very polished look, we wet the wood with tap water using clean cotton rags. This is done to raise the grain of the wood.

▼ 32. The finish of the interiors is just as important as that of the exterior. Therefore, the insides of the drawers are cleaned. Alcohol is applied with a cotton rag to remove the surface dirt and soften the grime. Any traces of dirt and stains are removed by scrubbing with a steel wool pad.

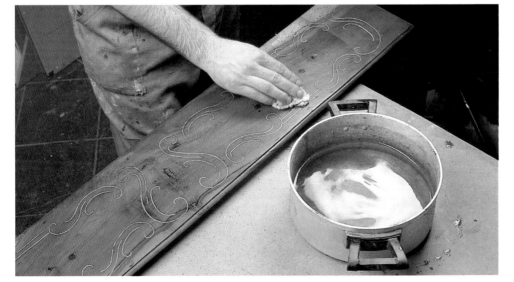

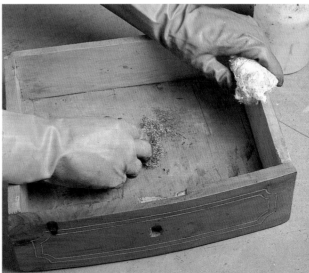

▲ **33.** After being cleaned and sanded, the interiors are protected from dirt by a coat of filler, applied with a cotton rag. This step should be carried out before beginning the finishing of the exterior of the chest of drawers. Otherwise, the finish will be exposed to possible stains and drips.

▲ **34.** A *relleno de cera* finish will be applied, consistent with the period of the piece. The surface is heavily waxed, using a cotton rag in a circular motion to make sure that the wax penetrates into the wood. When the wood is filled with wax, a last pass is made in the direction of the wood grain, and then the piece is left to dry.

◄ **35.** Pumice and powdered wax are sprinkled over the surface. A clean pad is dampened with alcohol and then lightly wet with wax. The mixture is applied with the pad by rubbing in a circular motion; this makes a paste the consistency of a filler that penetrates the wood. The step is repeated, with a smaller amount of ingredients, until the pores of the wood are completely filled. The last coat is always applied in the direction of the grain of the wood in order to eliminate any possible marks.

▼ **36.** When the piece has been given its final finish and the resulting color of the wood can be seen, the final touching up is done. An alcohol-based stain is applied with a picture retouching brush to the small areas that need it. The color is blended by tapping it lightly with the pad of a finger.

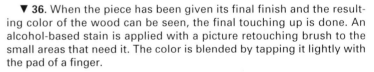

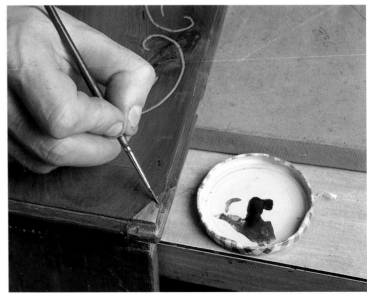

▶ **37.** The wood is polished by buffing it with a cotton cloth. Finally, the hardware is cleaned and replaced. We return the pulls to their original places, centered relative to the decorative inlay. This simple step helps to reestablish some of the old proportions of this chest.

▶ **38.** The top surfaces have neither marks nor stains. The wood has been given a natural and lasting finish that conditions it and is stylistically appropriate to the period of the furniture piece.

Mirror

S ometimes the restoration of an object can result in a complete transformation. In this exercise, we are faced with a situation that is quite common with certain types of furniture: sets and objects made by combining parts belonging to other pieces of furniture.

Here, a wall-hung mirror with a period frame, with an added decorative piece of a vaguely modernist style, was combined with a dressing table. The set was made to match by applying a heavy coat of black paint. A preliminary inspection and the later intervention confirmed the combination of unrelated objects.

We focus the restoration on the mirror, which turned out to have been gilded originally. Therefore, we will proceed to restore it to its original state by gilding it.

▲ The wood dressing table is painted black, and the top is covered with a piece of marble. This piece formed part of a set composed of the dressing table and wall-hung mirror.

▲ The mirror is the other part of the set. Upon first inspection, the carved decorative motifs differ notably from those of the dressing table. Nevertheless, the color and finish of this piece correspond to that of the other piece in the set, the dressing table.

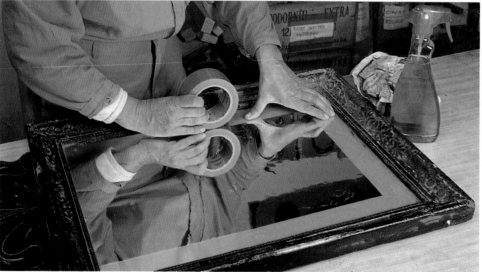

◀ 1. The process begins with the mirror, because it seems to be the piece that requires the most work. The first step is a thorough cleaning of the mirror with a glass cleaner and a clean cotton cloth. The edges are then protected by applying adhesive tape for glass.

◀ **2.** Bubble wrap, covering the entire surface of the glass, is applied with masking tape over the glass tape. A chemical solvent is applied with a brush to remove the thick coats of paint. It is important to protect your hands with neoprene gloves and to use a respirator.

▶ **3.** The chemical solvent is left to work until the painted surface begins to show a soft and wrinkled surface. Several tests are made to verify that the solvent will pull off the thick coats of paint.

▶ **4.** The solvent is removed with a paint scraper in the straight and smooth areas. In the parts with moldings, a graver helps remove the chemical from the corners and grooves. The excess stripper is removed from the flat areas with a cotton rag soaked in alcohol; these areas are then scrubbed with a steel wool pad.

◀ **5.** The complicated molding pieces and carvings in the corners are scraped with the graver, and the remnants of paint are removed by scrubbing with a cotton rag soaked in alcohol; these areas are then brushed. A flat brush with the bristles cut short is used to do the work of a scrub brush, but is much softer.

▲ 6. Once the frame is stripped and completely clean, the observation made during the preliminary inspection is proven correct. The frame does not match the style of the dressing table. Its original color was not black: Judging by the undercoat, it was gilded. The wavy carved ornament at the top does not match the molding pieces and flower motifs on the rest of the frame, and it is made of a different kind of wood.

Based on these conclusions, we will proceed to remove the decorative piece and return the frame to its original state.

▲ 7. The chipped and damaged areas are repaired by using a spatula to apply a commercial filler the same color as the base coat.

◀ 8. The repaired areas are thoroughly sanded with 100-grit sandpaper to shape the edge. Then, it is sanded with 150-grit paper until the surface is smooth.

▼ 9. In order to return the frame to its original state, gold leaf will have to be applied. To do so it is necessary to prepare the base with an acrylic undercoat applied with a brush. The color of the base coat gives depth to the gold leaf. In this case, we have chosen a red-toned acrylic color similar to that of the natural base coat that was traditionally used.

▼ 10. When the acrylic base coat is dry, a commercial gold leaf size is applied only on the areas to be gilded. The mixture acts as an adhesive and fixative for gold leaf.

Gilding can be applied either as gold leaf or painted in liquid form; the choice will depend on the value of the object.

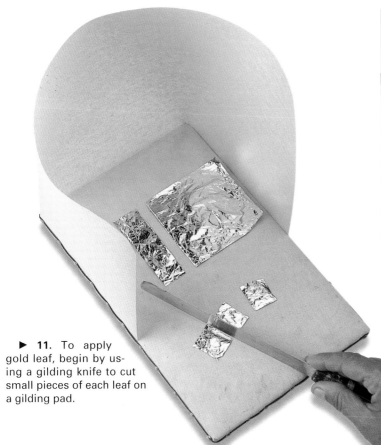

▶ **11.** To apply gold leaf, begin by using a gilding knife to cut small pieces of each leaf on a gilding pad.

▲ **12.** The small pieces of gold leaf are picked up with a special gilding brush called a polonaise. It is rubbed on the back of the hand to create enough static electricity to attract the gold leaf. A small amount of petroleum jelly can also be applied to the hand and rubbed with the brush until it is lightly coated, for better adhesion of the gold leaf to the brush.

▶ **13.** The piece of leaf is transferred with the brush to the part of the frame coated with the adhesive product. Place the piece so that it slightly overlaps the piece of gold leaf next to it, being especially careful not to leave a space or crack between them. Keep in mind that once the gold leaf has come in contact with the adhesive it is impossible to move.

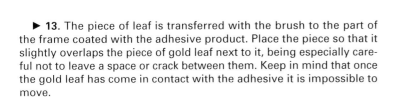

▼ **14.** Rub with a thick sable hair paintbrush to get a good bond between the leaf and the various moldings and carved borders.

▼ **15.** The poor quality of this frame, however, merits a simpler and less expensive gilding than with gold leaf. Therefore, we will use a metallic paint. This is prepared by mixing gold leaf powder and varnish (both commercially available) in a container. The proportions will depend on the desired thickness of the gilding. The mixture is applied to the entire frame with a brush.

▲ 16. This gilding makes the object look shiny and new; so when the mixture of varnish and powdered metal is dry, it will be aged using an antiquing technique. This is done by applying a coat of asphaltum with a brush, after thinning it to the required transparency.

▲ 17. The color of the asphaltum is blended by wiping with cotton strands or a rag.

► 18. When the stain is dry, we lightly rub the surface of the frame with steel wool. This procedure removes some of the finish from the raised areas, simulating the wear caused by handling and the passage of time. The reddish color of the base coat will come through in the areas most worn by rubbing.

▼ 20. An aged gold color is created by brushing on shellac that has been lightly tinted with a red alcohol-based stain.

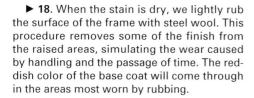

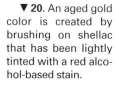

▼ 19. Scrubbing with a cotton rag soaked in solvent will simulate light wear on the smooth parts of the frame.

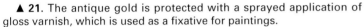

▲ **21.** The antique gold is protected with a sprayed application of gloss varnish, which is used as a fixative for paintings.

▲ **22.** Finally, all traces of chemicals and gold leaf are removed from the mirror glass with a scraper. Then it is thoroughly cleaned with a glass cleaner.

▶ **23.** The project results in an object that looks very different from the way it looked before restoration. It has been stripped of additions of doubtful stylistic affiliation and separated from a piece of furniture that was originally never part of a set. The frame has been restored to its original look.

Chest with Marquetry Work

It is sometimes necessary to restore objects that at first glance do not seem to require it. In this case, it seemed that the main problem with the piece was nothing more than a layer of grime. The evaluation process, however, revealed the presence of insect activity, as well as the unhappy results of an old restoration: filler of a darker color than the original wood, and poorly repaired marquetry with warped pieces that were close to coming off. We also noted a problem that is very common to storage pieces with doors; they were so far out of alignment that it was impossible to close them. The misalignment of the doors occurred from the incorrect placement of the hinges that attached them to the chest. Therefore, we proceeded to remove them and to reattach them later. The marquetry work done with woods of various colors and placed in different directions could have presented a great problem during the process of repair. An intermediate color from among all the woods was chosen as a solution. When it came to the direction of the wood grain, we thought it best to hand sand in the direction of the majority of them. To complete the project, the chest was given the kind of final finish that would accentuate the quality of the inlay work that was on all surfaces.

▲ A sideboard chest with decorative marquetry on the sides and doors. This piece has traces of old restorations that are easily seen in the dark filler in the wood. Areas of warped veneer and loss of material on some outside corners can be seen. The doors do not close and sag toward the middle, which indicates that the hinges are misaligned.

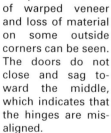

▲ 1. The first step is to detach the moving parts of the chest, removing the two doors. The hinges are removed with great care to avoid damaging the inlay underneath. A wooden wedge is placed between the hinge and the marquetry and is gently tapped at the opposite end with a nylon-headed hammer. This way the nails that hold it will begin to come out.

◀ 2. When the hinge has come away from the surface of the wood, a metal scraper is inserted to protect the marquetry, and a slight lever motion is applied while tapping a screwdriver with the nylon-headed hammer. This way the nails of the hinges are loosened.

▲ 3. We remove the nails by pulling them out with pliers. If the removal is difficult, the pliers can be braced against the hinge, but never against the wood, which would be marred. When applying force with the pliers, care should be taken not to break the heads off the nails, because they will be used in the reassembly of the chest.

▶ 4. It is noted that the chest is infested by insects and that they are still active in some areas. Because they were confined to specific areas, they are eliminated by injecting an insecticide into the holes.

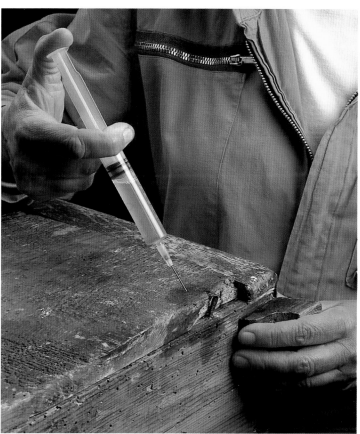

▼ 5. The surfaces of the chest are stripped with alcohol. Alcohol is the appropriate solvent for inlay work, because it evaporates quickly and does not swell the thin sheets of wood. We apply alcohol with clean cotton strands or a rag and then rub with steel wool. The direction of the sanding will be dictated by the direction of the grain of the majority of the marquetry work.

▼ 6. We proceed to repair the pieces of raised marquetry work. White PVA glue is applied under the thin sheet of wood using a palette knife. The excess is wiped off with a clean cotton rag.

▲ **7.** We flatten the veneer by pressing it with the point of a hot iron. Several passes are made to totally evaporate the water contained in the glue and to get a good bond.

▶ **8.** The repaired area is hand sanded with 100-grit sandpaper in the direction of the grain of the glued veneer. This will remove traces of glue and make it level with the rest of the wood top.

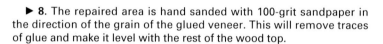

◀ **9.** Several corners are missing material. This particular one was previously repaired and has a thick layer of glue. Before starting the repair work, all traces of glue and dirt are removed by prying with a gouge; then the surface of the wood is smoothed by lightly carving with the same tool.

▼ **10.** The repair is made with a two-part liquid resin. To build up an angle it is necessary to make a mold at the corner, for which we use two pieces of wood cut slightly larger than the break. One of the surfaces of the wood is rubbed with paraffin.

▲ **11.** One of the blocks is attached to the back of the piece; it is nailed with two brads. The waxed surface faces the inside.

▲ **12.** The second block is attached to form a corner with the first and is nailed with two brads at one end. The bottom edge and the other end are attached to the side of the chest with adhesive tape. This way we do not mark or puncture the marquetry. Then, the two-part resin is mixed according to the instructions on the package and is poured into the mold that was just constructed.

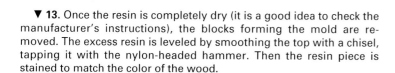

▼ **13.** Once the resin is completely dry (it is a good idea to check the manufacturer's instructions), the blocks forming the mold are removed. The excess resin is leveled by smoothing the top with a chisel, tapping it with the nylon-headed hammer. Then the resin piece is stained to match the color of the wood.

► **14.** Once the marquetry work has been stripped, it is of a lighter color than it seemed to be on first inspection. The old restoration filled the holes caused by the insects with a hard, dark-colored filler. This is the reason the finish is so unattractive now. To remedy this situation, the old filler is removed by scraping out each hole with an awl.

▲ **15.** With the old filler gone, the holes are filled with new putty that matches the wood. In order to choose a color that will go well with the different woods that make up the marquetry work, we need to see what the color will be after the final finish. To do so, the surface is dampened with alcohol applied with clean cotton rags.

▶ **16.** The commercial filler is applied with a spatula. Given the great number and size of the holes, the coat will be liberally applied in the area needing repair, not hole by hole.

▲ **17.** When the filler is dry, we hand sand the entire surface with 100-grit sandpaper, following the direction of the grain of the majority of the pieces of marquetry work to eliminate the excess filler.

▶ **18.** The chest is then sanded with 150-grit sandpaper to remove any possible marks and scratches caused by successive sandings and to achieve a fine smooth surface.

▲ **19.** All surfaces are thoroughly cleaned with a vacuum cleaner using a brush attachment.

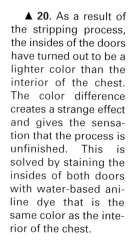

▶ **21.** The water base of the stain raises the grain of the wood. This is removed by vigorously scrubbing in the direction of the wood grain with a soft natural fiber brush (or esparto grass), taking special care not to scratch or mark the wood.

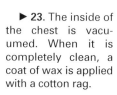

▲ **20.** As a result of the stripping process, the insides of the doors have turned out to be a lighter color than the interior of the chest. The color difference creates a strange effect and gives the sensation that the process is unfinished. This is solved by staining the insides of both doors with water-based aniline dye that is the same color as the interior of the chest.

◀ **22.** The backs of the doors are waxed using cotton strands or a rag.

▶ **23.** The inside of the chest is vacuumed. When it is completely clean, a coat of wax is applied with a cotton rag.

▲ **24.** Hard waxes are used to repair small imperfections in specific areas that have just a few holes. We choose wax sticks as close as possible in color and tone to the kinds of wood that make up the table.

▲ **25.** A small quantity of wax is kneaded with the fingers to soften it, and we press it into each imperfection with a wooden spatula.

◀ **26.** When the wax is dry, the backs of the doors and the interior of the chest are polished by vigorously buffing with a clean cotton cloth.

▼ **27.** The backside of furniture is not usually finished. Staining it will help it stay clean and renew the wood. In this case, we apply a coat of asphaltum lightly thinned with turpentine.

▲ **28.** The final finish on the piece consists of a *mechado*. This is a procedure that imparts a warm satiny appearance to the wood. We apply a generous amount of wax with cotton strands or cheesecloth.

▲ **29**. The wax is spread until it has completely filled the pores of the wood. Several coats are applied if needed.

▶ **31**. Then, two or three coats of shellac are applied with a pad. This is always applied in the direction of the grain until a uniform gloss is achieved.

▼ **32**. Finally, the shellac is covered with a last coat of wax applied in the direction of the grain. It is burnished with a soft, natural fiber brush.

▲ **30**. When the wax is completely dry, it is rubbed in the direction of the wood grain using a soft natural fiber brush (or esparto grass) until we create a glossy surface.

▼ **33**. The grime on the metal parts (keyhole and hinges) is removed by rubbing the surface with steel wool.

▲ **34.** The completely cleaned metal parts are waxed with the same paste wax that was applied to the wood.

▲ **35.** We lay the hinges on the chest, placing them so that they will hold the doors correctly. A small nail is used to mark the place where the hinges will be nailed, while the wood is protected with a thick piece of paper.

▲ **36.** A hole is made in the wood with a gimlet at the spot previously marked with the nail.

▶ **37.** The metal parts, in this case the keyhole, are attached with the original nails. The gimlet handle is used to protect the metal and nails while the keyhole is attached.

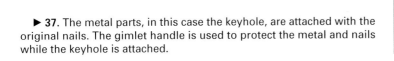

◄ 38. We polish the chest, buffing it with a cotton or wool cloth. Thanks to the *mechado* technique, we get a deep satiny shine.

▼ 39. The result of the restoration is a piece of furniture that reflects the quality of the marquetry work. At the same time, it has become a useful storage piece again because of the repair of the doors that would not close before.

Modernist-Style Wardrobe

*S*ometimes a restoration project is focused solely on the finish of the wood. A furniture piece may be in perfect condition when it comes to the wood, but its finish may be very poor.

Antique furniture pieces usually retain their original finish, which is by nature fragile and deteriorates with the passage of time.

A waxed finish has a tendency to collect dust and grime from its surroundings, turning slightly opaque or holding dust in the seams, joints, and moldings. Shellac finishes tend to darken with the passage of time. Added to this are marks, scratches, small scrapes, and water splashes caused by the wear and tear of daily use, or a poor state of conservation caused by excessive exposure to light or direct sunlight.

The style and period, as well as the original finish that is still on the piece, all will indicate the restoration process that is needed.

▲ **1.** The restoration begins by removing the parts of the piece of furniture, marking their placement and carefully storing all of the hardware. Then the wood is completely stripped using a clean rag soaked with alcohol. Since we are dealing with old shellac, the alcohol will act as a solvent without damaging the wood.

◄ A Modernist-style wardrobe made of walnut. Despite continuous use, the piece shows no damage to either the structure or the wood itself. The only effect of the passage of time is the darkening of the coat of shellac that covers it.

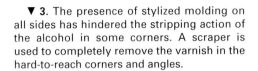
◄ 2. We proceed by sanding the entire surface of the wardrobe. This will be done by hand with 100-grit sandpaper, and we will finish sanding with 150-grit sandpaper, until we achieve a perfectly smooth surface.

▼ 3. The presence of stylized molding on all sides has hindered the stripping action of the alcohol in some corners. A scraper is used to completely remove the varnish in the hard-to-reach corners and angles.

◄ 4. Once the old darkened coat of varnish has been removed, the finishing process begins. First, we proceed to fill the pores of the wood with shellac. Several coats are applied with cotton rags soaked in shellac until the pores are completely filled. It is important to keep in mind that a minimum of two or three coats will be required to begin to fill the pores.

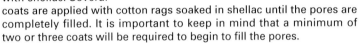

► 5. When the shellac is completely dry, we sprinkle some finely ground pumice over the surface of the wood (a saltshaker can be helpful).

▲ 6. The rubbing pad is charged with shellac and some drops of alcohol on the inside, and a couple of drops of liquid petroleum jelly are added to the outside to help the rubbing on the surface.

▲ 7. A pastelike consistency results from rubbing with circular motions on the surface, which has been dusted with pumice. The paste penetrates the wood under light but firm pressure. The rubbing pad is recharged with alcohol, and the pumice is sprinkled as many times as we think necessary until the pores of the wood are filled.

◄ 8. Traces of paste and all other marks are removed by making a final pass in the direction of the wood grain with the rubbing pad soaked with alcohol.

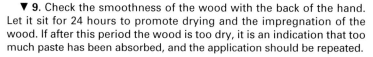

▼ 9. Check the smoothness of the wood with the back of the hand. Let it sit for 24 hours to promote drying and the impregnation of the wood. If after this period the wood is too dry, it is an indication that too much paste has been absorbed, and the application should be repeated.

▲ **10.** We finish by varnishing the wardrobe with shellac. This step must be done in a room that has a stable temperature between 60 and 65°F (15–18°C), without too much humidity, and above all is free of dust and dirt, because this is a very delicate finish. The rubbing pad is charged with more alcohol than shellac and all the surfaces are wiped in overlapping figure eight motions. As each new coat is applied, the proportion of alcohol is reduced and the proportion of shellac is increased, while the overlapping motions increase in size until the final coat is applied in the direction of the wood grain.

▶ **11.** Excess oil left from the application of the shellac is removed with a pad soaked in alcohol. Once the shellac is dry, the hardware is attached, in this case the two door pulls. With this finish, we have completed a piece of furniture with the original wood tone using the period varnish, where all the beauty of the austere marquetry work can be appreciated.

Glossary

a

aniline. A generic name for pigments derived from organic synthesis; they form colorful dyes that are transparent and not very lightfast.

b

biodeterioration. Damage, deterioration, or changes in wood caused by biological agents.

bleaching. Changing the color of wood, usually to a lighter tone, by applying chemical substances.

board. A flat piece of wood used in furniture construction.

burnishing. A technique used to prepare wood for finishing, consisting of a thorough preliminary sanding, and then a wetting with tap water to raise the grain. The grain is then removed by rubbing it with a block or piece of cork to give the wood a polished finish.

c

carnuba. A gray-colored substance that is harder and more fragile than beeswax. Extracted from a certain variety of palm tree, it adds hardness when mixed with beeswax.

caustic soda. Sodium hydroxide. A highly corrosive water-soluble chemical used for stripping solid pine.

chisel. A steel tool used for carving wood. It has a flat wide shape, is sharpened at one end, and has a wood handle at the other.

clamp. A plastic or steel tool used to hold two pieces of glued wood so that they bond to one another completely.

contour gauge. A tool with a row of movable metal pins that is used to copy profiles from parts and molding.

d

decant. To very slowly pour a mixture of various ingredients while controlling the amount.

dovetail. A joint made of a series of trapezoidal pins and slots that keeps the pieces from pulling apart.

dowel. A small cylindrical piece of wood, sometimes slightly conical, for holding and reinforcing joints.

e

encaustic. A glossy finish achieved by applying liquid wax to wood until it is supersaturated and then buffing.

f

fill. To reinforce or smooth wood by filling voids or impregnating them with adhesives.

frame. A structure to which something can be mounted, such as panels in the case of furniture.

French polish. A finish achieved by applying shellac to fill the pores of the wood, then dusting with pumice, which is rubbed with a rubbing pad charged with alcohol, and then lacquering the surface.

g

gilding cushion. A tool used for holding and cutting gold leaf during the gilding process. It consists of a wood rectangle approximately 6 inches by 9 inches by 1/2 inch (15 × 22 × 1 cm) with a layer of padding on top covered with a chamois. The chamois is slightly rough and holds the gold leaf in place.

gilding knife. A tool with a long narrow blade and a wood handle. It looks like a common knife but has no cutting edge. It is used for smoothing and cutting gold leaf.

gimlet. A tool used for making holes in wood and similar materials. Consists of a steel shank with a screw thread at one end and a handle at the other for turning the tool.

glue (to). To bond two parts together using an adhesive.

gold leaf. Very fine sheets of beaten gold sold in 3¹/₂-inch (8-cm) and 5¹/₂-inch (14-cm) squares in booklets. The sheets are separated by protective pages.

gouge. A chisel with a curved blade.

graver. A tool formed by a piece of pointed steel with a wood handle. Used for scraping.

h

handsaw. A cutting tool consisting of a steel blade with teeth and a wood handle attached to one end.

hinge. Hardware made of two connected pieces, usually steel, that rotate on a pin. Used for hanging doors in a frame, it allows them to swing.

hot air gun. An electric appliance that blows hot air and is used for stripping paint and varnish. It has controls for speed and temperature.

hot glue gun. An electric appliance used for applying hot glue, which is usually sold in sticks.

hygroscopic. Describes a material whose moisture content tends to stay the same as the humidity of its surroundings.

i

incision. A cut made in the surface of wood.

inlay. A surface decoration consisting of pieces of wood, bone, metal, or other materials inserted in incisions made in solid wood.

j

jack plane. A tool similar to a plane, but larger and with a handle, which allows the application of greater force.

join (joinery). Attaching pieces of wood to each other with joints like the mortise and tenon.

k

knot. Hard formation occurring at the point where a branch intersects with a tree trunk.

m

marking gauge. Instrument consisting of a small block with two adjustable bars and a steel point at one end going through it at a right angle. Used for making parallel lines on a piece of wood.

marquetry. Decoration made by gluing different pieces of wood veneers or other materials on the wood's surface, creating a smooth, even surface.

mechado. A finish consisting of several coats of wax that completely fill the pores of the wood and that is polished with esparto grass or a soft natural fiber brush. Then several coats of shellac are applied that, once dry, are covered with a last coat of wax that is then buffed.

metallic paint. A fine metallic powder that looks like gold and that is applied in a transparent medium.

molding. Element with uniform relief and profile used as decoration. Appears in both simple and compound forms.

mortise. Joint or square hole made in a piece of wood so that it can be joined to a tenon.

n

nail lifter. Steel lever with a split at one end that is used to grab nail heads to extract them.

nail set. A steel punch about 2 inches (10 cm) long with a flat or slightly rounded point. Used to inset nail heads below the surface.

p

paraffin. A solid, white substance composed of a mixture of hydrocarbons, obtained by distilling lignite and coal.

pathology. Study of the possible disorders of wood as a material.

patina. Tone, color, and quality that develop on the surface of old objects through to the passage of time.

pheromone. Sexual hormone given off by certain animals to attract the opposite sex of the same species.

plane. Tool made of a hard wood block with a slanted steel cutter that protrudes slightly. Used to remove wood material.

plasticity. The malleable quality of certain materials.

polonaise. A very flat brush made of a uniform (straight) line of bristles fixed between two pieces of cardboard about 1 inch to 3 inches (3 to 8 cm) wide. Used to pick up gold leaf to place it on the surface to be gilded.

r

raised grain. A group of fibers on the wood surface that stands up above the grain. They become raised when the wood is wet.

rasp. A type of file with large, protruding teeth. Used for removing wood, smoothing, and rounding edges.

red base coat. A reddish-orange colored mixture of natural iron oxide clay, calcium, and magnesium silicates. Used as a mordant base for water gilding. It has been replaced by synthetic mixtures.

relative humidity. The relation expressed as a percentage of the amount of water vapor that exists in a volume of air and the quantity there could be if it were saturated.

relleno de cera. A finish achieved by waxing the surface of the wood, dusting it with pumice, and then creating a paste by rubbing the surface with a rag soaked in alcohol and covered with wax.

reparation. To replace an area or missing piece.

resin. A natural (comes from different trees) or artificial (chemical compounds) substance used as an adhesive or as a component of varnish.

respirator. A mask that covers the nose and mouth to filter dust and harmful gases.

rings. Annual growth marks in tree trunks formed in the spring and fall.

rubbing pad. Small wad of fabric wrapped in a cloth. Used to apply a fine coat of varnish. Rubbing spreads the varnish and polishes at the same time.

s

sander. A power tool with a rotating disk or a belt that allows the quick sanding of large surfaces.

sanding. The action of rubbing a surface with sandpaper to make it smooth.

sanding block. Wood or cork block to which sandpaper can be easily affixed. Used for hand sanding.

saturation. When a material is completely impregnated by another or when it can absorb no more of it.

saw. A tool consisting of a steel blade with sharp teeth that is set into a handle or frame. Used to cut wood by moving back and forth repeatedly.

scraper. A blade with a handle. Used for scraping surfaces.

scraping. A method for stripping surfaces using different types of blades (straight or shaped) appropriate for solid wood.

shellac. A delicate resin that comes from the East Indies. Available in flakes of various yellow to brown tones or in white bars; it is soluble in alcohol or water and slightly alkaline.

size. Varnish made of linseed oil with additives. Slow drying and highly corrosive. Used in gilding when the gold leaf is to be left matte and not polished.

stain. Paint of liquid consistency and very fine pigment that colors without covering, thereby showing the quality and grain of the wood.

stripping. To eliminate layers of paint or varnish that cover a wood surface.

supersaturated solution. Solution of one component dissolved in another than cannot absorb any more and begins to precipitate.

tenon. The end of a piece of wood, cut down to a cylindrical or rectangular section, which allows it to be inserted and fixed in a matching hole in another piece of wood.

tourniquet. Clamping system consisting of a thick cord wrapped around the surfaces to be held. Pressure is applied by twisting with a piece of wood.

varnish. A gum or resin solution (natural or synthetic) in solvent that is applied to a surface to form a more or less shiny, transparent, and impermeable surface.

veneer. A very thin sheet of wood that is applied as a covering or decoration.

W

wax. Mineral, animal, or vegetable substance (having characteristics in common) used as a final coat on wood.

wood borer. Parasitic insect that lives in or on wood. Some species also consume the wood.

wood grain. Veins or fibers in wood that all lay in the same direction.

Bibliography
and Acknowledgments

Allen, S. *Classic Finishing Techniques.* Sterling. New York. 1995.

Blaser, W. *Joint & Connections: Furniture Design and Its Background.* Birkhauser. Cambridge, MA. 1992.

Brumbaugh, J. *Wood Furniture: Finishing, Refinishing, Repairing.* Mcmillan. New York. 1992.

Buchanan, G. *The Illustrated Handbook of Furniture Restoration.* Trafalgar. Vermont. 1996.

Creffield, J. *Wood Destroying Insects.* Intl. Spec. Bk. Portland, OR. 1996.

Eaton, R. *Wood: Decay, Pests & Protection.* Chapman & Hall. New York. 1993.

Fine Woodworking Magazine Editors. *Veneering, Marquetry & Inlay.* Taunton. Newton, CT. 1996.

Gloag, John. *A Complete Dictionary of Furniture.* Overlook Press. New York. 1991.

Hayward, H. *World Furniture: An Illustrated History.* Random House Value. New York. 1988.

Hoadley, R. *Identifying Wood: A Practical Handbook for Craftsmen.* Taunton. Newton, CT. 1990.

Joyce, E. *Encyclopedia of Furniture Making.* Sterling. New York. 1989.

Katz, S. *Hispanic Furniture: An American Collection.* Archit CT. Stamford, CT. 1986.

Lincoln, Wm. *A Complete Manual of Wood Veneering.* Linden Pub. Fresno, CA. 1995.

Lincoln, Wm. *A World of Woods in Color.* Linden Pub. Fresno, CA. 1991.

Lucie-Smith, E. *Furniture: A Concise History.* Thames Hudson. New York. 1985.

Rodd, J. *Repairing and Restoring Antique Furniture.* Sterling. New York. 1995.

Rubia, J. *Classical European Furniture Design.* Random House. New York. 1989.

Square, D. *The Veneering Book.* Taunton. Newton, CT. 1995.

To Magda Gassó for her friendship, continual help, and support over many years.
To Marc Salvador for his infinite patience and unconditional support in all the projects that I undertake.
To Josep Pascual for the advice and experience he has passed to me.

Eva Pascual

To Mireia Campanyá for the valuable collaboration in the section on marquetry and for her knowledge and assistance in the section on species of wood.
To Mercedes González for her vast knowledge of gold leafing.

Anna Jover, Josep Maria Miret, and Eva Pascual